Donate Less to the I.R.S.

Donate Less to the I.R.S.

ANTIQUE COLLECTOR'S AND SELLER'S TAX REDUCTION GUIDE

D. Larry Crumbley, Ph.D., CPA
and
Jerry Curtis, Ph.D.

THE VESTAL PRESS LTD
VESTAL, NEW YORK 13850

Composition by
Eastern Graphics
Binghamton, New York 13901

Cover design by
John Marshall
The Art Department
Binghamton, New York 13901

Library of Congress Cataloging in Publication Data

Crumbley, D. Larry
Donate less to the I.R.S.

Bibliography: p.
Includes index.
1. Tax planning—United States. 2. Antiques—Taxation—United States.
I. Curtis, Jerry, 1941– II. Title. III. Title: Donate less to the I.R.S.
KF6297.C78 343.7305'246 81-21806
ISBN 0-911572-23-6 347.3035246 AACR2

"NO MAN IS UNDER THE SMALLEST OBLIGATION, MORAL OR OTHERWISE, TO SO ARRANGE HIS AFFAIRS AS TO ENABLE THE REVENUE SERVICE TO PUT THE LARGEST POSSIBLE SHOVEL INTO HIS STORES."

. . . Lord Clyde

Collecting more taxes than absolutely necessary is robbery.

. . . Calvin Coolidge

Table of Contents

CHAPTER 1

Introduction

The recent increased interest in our own past coupled with the desire to own things that are practical, beautiful, and unique has caused the field of antiques to grow almost unbelievably. In recent years investors have actively entered the field of antiques. The antique market is open to anyone who wishes to buy and sell. Generally, there are no strict organizations, no closed shops, no brokers or intermediaries who "fix" prices. No longer is antique collecting considered to be a pastime for those who have nothing else to do. When a single porcelain statue can sell for $50,000 and antique firms employ hundreds of people to satisfy the need of the collector or investor, all must agree that antiques are big business! For example, the Metropolitan Museum of Art paid $1 million plus $300,000 in rare Greek coins at an auction in Switzerland in 1972 for a vase fashioned in Greece around 500 B.C. By having a knowledge of some basic tax and finance principles, an investor, collector, or dealer is in a much better position to earn the maximum return on his investment.

Benjamin Franklin made famous the quotation "Nothing is certain except death and taxes." May we add the certainty of increasing antique values? Although this may not be entirely true, it is probable in view of the past performance records of most antiques. Perhaps, in light of current governmental policies old Ben Franklin should have also forecast ever increasing taxes. It is true that as the years go by a larger and larger portion of every tax dollar is claimed by federal, state, and local taxes.

Clearly, the future is going to find an ever increasing portion of your antique investments being lost to taxes. That is, *unless you know what to do about the problem and know how to deal with it!* People are often amazed at the tremendous sums of money which the various governments collect each year due to no reason other than poor tax planning on the part of taxpayers. These are sums which could have and should have been legally avoided. Our government expects not one cent more than what is legally due. If the law provides certain techniques and methods of avoiding burdensome taxes, these provisions should be used whenever and to whatever extent possible.

This book is about tax laws. We did not write these laws—we can only try to interpret them. We do not manufacture the long words—your congressmen do. Each year the laws become more and more complex. Write and complain to your congressman. One should be able to understand the tax law without a C.P.A. certificate. Encourage the legislators to write understandable tax laws. As an example of what we mean, there is one sentence in the tax law which is 564 words long, and another is more than 400 words long. By contrast, Lincoln's Gettysburg Address is only about 480 words, and the whole of the Ten Commandments is shorter!

Many others have complained more articulately than we are able to do. Albert Einstein, while commenting on completing his own tax return said, "This is too difficult for a mathematician. It takes a philosopher. The hardest thing in the world to understand is the income tax."

An important fact in this book is that we try to present an idea in very simple language initially and then go into more detail. The book is written so that each part is relatively independent of the rest. If part of the book does not interest you, skip that part and go on to another part. The authors will not be offended and you will save valuable time.

Since some people will have a keen interest in that particular subject we will explain the concept in more detail. Warning: You may have to read the section two or three times. The worst thing that a *tax* writer can do is to write a superficial section and leave you dangling for more complete and probably more correct information. Think of our book as trying to "educate" antique buffs to the complexity of our tax laws and how to use them successfully.

Bear in mind that in some sections we will barely scratch the surface. You may have to consult a certified public accountant or lawyer to understand the subject in depth. Take a copy of this book to your counselor, and let him or her explain it to you.

Yes, taxation is boring—we admit it. We hate to fill out our own tax returns, especially when we know that the average taxpayer works at least four months out of the year for the government. That is how long it takes to pay the taxes for federal, state, and local budgets. As one observer has said, "A taxpayer is someone who does not have to take a civil service examination to work for the government."

Education is painful and tax planning is difficult. Do not expect to read this book like an entertaining novel. There are other entertaining (and some fiction) pieces in the literature about antiques, but we try to deal strictly with facts, not fiction. The tax facts are extremely complex.

Consider this book as a guide to a marvelously complex system. Ignore that which is not useful and prepare an itinerary of the useful sites that you wish to visit. Then visit your own tax counselor and ask him or her how your itinerary will match your strengths and weaknesses.

A few final words about tax savings and investments in general. Remember that all tax savings are top dollars savings. These dollars would have been taxed at the highest rate for your income bracket, and do not forget that any state income tax (also at the highest rate) is to be added to this figure.

Antique investments are different from money investments in that they are valuable and probably beautiful, too. However, they do not pay dividends.

But remember, an investment in antiques is not worthwhile economically unless it appears that the rate of return from the investment will be at least equal to that which could be earned from other investment alternatives (e.g., bank interest, stocks, bonds, real estate, or commodities). That is, the potential gain from a hobby-related investment should equal or exceed any potential income from an alternative investment before the hobby-related investment is worthwhile economically. For example, an antique investor should consider the risk from robbery, the expenses of keeping antiques, *plus* the lost interest that would have accrued from an alternative investment (commonly known as opportunity cost).

One has to be very careful in evaluating wooden decoys; they can range anywhere in today's market from $25 for a simple one to thousands of dollars for particularly desirable pieces. The I.R.S. understands full well such appreciation in value, and works hard to make certain that Uncle Sam gets all that he thinks he has coming. Your understanding of tax matters will make certain you don't have to give Uncle any more than he's entitled to get. (Photo courtesy of Mapes Auctioneers/Appraisers, Vestal, New York)

CHAPTER 2

Honesty is the Best Policy

A few years ago, the press widely publicized a quotation by a stockbroker in Atlanta who said, "The difference between tax avoidance and tax evasion is five years and $10,000." Tax avoidance is the word used to describe tax reduction methods that are permitted by the law. Tax evasion is any method of reducing taxes that is not permitted by the law, for which the law provides heavy penalties. Avoidance is "playing the game" according to the rules. Evasion is breaking the rules of the "tax game"—which is treated as a criminal offense.

Without some strong penalties to "encourage" taxpayers to pay the taxes the law requires, many citizens would just not pay. Despite the ritualistic statements by each successive I.R.S. Commissioner about our marvelous "self-assessment" method of taxation, the system is really based on fear. The public is simply afraid that if they don't pay what the I.R.S. says they owe, then the I.R.S. will attach their salaries, impound their property, and put them in jail. This is precisely what the tax law writers in Congress wanted to achieve. They knew the I.R.S. would have to have a variety of penalties to encourage us to be honest.

The I.R.S. has civil as well as criminal sanctions for certain violations of the tax laws. Civil sanctions are assessed in addition to the tax liability, but they are not considered to be felonies—i.e., criminal violations. These civil penalties include (1) the 5% per month delinquency penalty for failure to file a return or a timely return—which is not to exceed 25%, (2) the 5% negligence penalty for negligence or intentional disregard of rules and regulations without the intent to defraud, (3) 50% of the interest payable on the portion of the underpayment attributable to negligence or intentional disregard, and (4) the 50% fraud penalty on an underpayment on any portion which is due to fraud. The purpose of this 50% non-criminal fraud penalty is to give the I.R.S. a strong civil sanction that can be imposed without all the time and expense usually required in the prosecution of a criminal violation of the laws. Ostensibly, the 50% fraud penalty is to "reimburse" the government for the cost of discovering and investigating fraudulent violations of the tax laws

The *criminal* sanctions provide punishment for severe offenses and generally involve imprisonment and/or fines. For example, a person who willfully attempts in any manner to evade or defeat a tax may, if found guilty of a felony and convicted, be fined not more than $10,000 and/or imprisoned not more than 5 years, together with the costs of prosecution. Both *civil* and *criminal* sanctions may be imposed for the same offense. The difference is often a matter of whether the I.R.S. wants to make a public example out of a particular tax evader or whether they just want to collect the money, or both. Generally, the I.R.S. prefers just to collect the taxes plus any non-criminal penalties the law permits, even though the taxpayer could be prosecuted for a criminal offense.

The burden and measure of proof differs in *criminal* and *civil* cases. In *criminal* cases, the I.R.S. must prove every facet of the offense and show guilt beyond a reasonable doubt. In case of fraud, the I.R.S. has the burden of establishing such fraud by clear and convincing evidence. A taxpayer should be acquitted if the evidence is equally consistent with innocence as with guilt.

Avoidance of taxes, on the other hand, is not a criminal offense. Any attempt by a taxpayer to avoid, reduce, minimize, or defer his taxes by legitimate means is permissible. The distinction between avoidance and evasion is a fine line, but a definite one.

A taxpayer who avoids taxes does not conceal or misrepresent. He shapes events to reduce or eliminate his tax liability and, upon the happening of the events, makes a complete disclosure. For example, a taxpayer may wish to "pull" expenses into this year. On December 30, he may write a check and send it to a charitable organization in order to obtain a charitable contribution deduction in December. Even though the check may not be cashed by the organization until around January 20, the deduction would be available in December. Or, the taxpayer may choose to purchase tax exempt municipal bonds instead of purchasing fully taxable corporate bonds.

Evasion, by contrast, involves deceit, subterfuge, camouflage, concealment, or an attempt to color or obscure events. For example, the taxpayer writes the check on December 30, but does not mail the check until January 5th to the charitable organization, or the taxpayer may have written the check in January and dated it in December. Other forms of subterfuge would be knowingly reporting 200 miles for a business trip instead of 120 miles, or taking turns in buying and deducting lunch expenses with another business acquaintance. Failing to report cash income is another form of subterfuge.

The willful attempt to evade or defeat any tax, or the willful attempt to evade or defeat the payment of any tax, constitute criminal offenses. Three elements are necessary for a criminal offense: (1) an additional tax is due and owing, (2) there is an attempt in any manner to evade or defeat any tax, and (3) the attempt is willful.

The I.R.S. must establish that, at the time the offense was committed, an additional tax was due and owing. In essence, the individual must owe more taxes than he reported. But the I.R.S. does not have to prove evasion of the full amount alleged in the indictment. It is sufficient to show that a substantial amount of the tax was evaded, and this proof need not be measured in terms

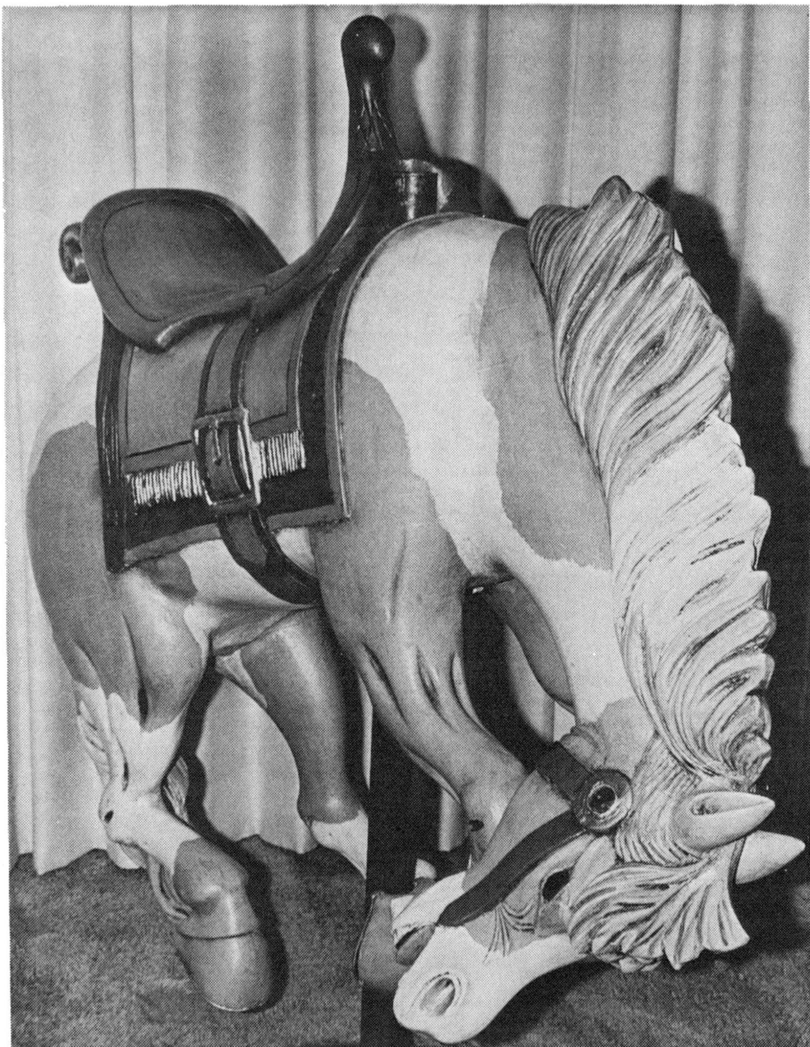

Carousel animals—horses, lions, giraffes, and other wooden carousel figures have taken enormous jumps in value, from a few dollars 20 years ago to thousands today, and many thousands in some cases! These dollar increases have not been lost on the I.R.S., so owners beware! Become aware of the implications of your collectibles and their values. (Photo courtesy of Marianne and David Stevens)

of gross or net income or by any particular percentage of the tax shown to be due and payable. (It is the current policy of the I.R.S. not to authorize assessment of any additional taxes and penalties during the time any criminal charges are pending, and to postpone any discussion or negotiation involving settlement of the *civil* liability.)

The phrase "attempt in any manner" does not mean that those whose efforts are unsuccessful have not committed the crime of willful *attempt.* The crime is complete when the attempt is made and nothing is changed by its success or failure. The criminal character of an offense lies, not in the failure to file a return or in the filing of a false return, but rather in the attempt to evade any tax. Thus, the term "attempt" implies some affirmative action or the commission of some overt act. The Supreme Court has given certain illustrations from which acts or conduct the attempt to evade or defeat any tax may be inferred: (1) keeping a double set of books, (2) making false entries, (3) alterations of invoices or documents, (4) destruction of books and records, (5) concealment of assets or covering up sources of income, and (6) the handling of one's affairs to avoid making the records that are usual in transactions of the kind.

Willfulness is an essential element of proof with respect to most criminal violations investigated by special agents. This word "willful" generally means an act done with a bad purpose; without justifiable excuse; stubbornly, obstinately, perversely. The Supreme Court indicates that this word characterizes an act done without grounds for believing it is lawful, or conduct marked by careless disregard whether or not one has the right so to act. The most laudable motive is no defense where the act committed is a crime committed with knowledge of the law. For example, a taxpayer may intentionally understate his income in order to have sufficient funds to support invalid parents. Although such motive may be admirable, he has specifically intended to evade payment of his income taxes. Wilfullness is a state of mind which is difficult to prove. Circumstantial evidence is frequently used to prove willfulness. The following acts have been used by courts to prove willfulness: (1) attempted bribery of a revenue agent, (2) visits to undisclosed safe deposit boxes after having been questioned about assets, (3) making false statements, (4) withholding records during investigation, and (5) influencing the testimony of prospective witnesses.

Ignorance of the law is a defense against criminal penalties, but is not a defense against civil penalties. Even though criminal tax evasion is difficult to prove, civil tax avoidance is not necessarily a financially painless alternative. But, at least the *avoidance of taxes* is not a criminal felony and does not carry the risk of a jail term. Thus, the *real* difference between tax evasion and tax avoidance is the possibility of a jail term and possible financial penalties in addition to any civil penalties.

Dealing only in cash will not necessarily allow you to hide income. The I.R.S. has many ways to catch you. To catch tax evaders, the I.R.S. has relied upon two traditional indirect methods of proving undisclosed income: (1) bank deposits and cash expenditures method and (2) net worth method. A recent court decision involving a medical practitioner should illustrate this first method.

Dr. Loophole was on a calendar year basis, and the I.R.S. charged him with willful evasion of income taxes for four years. To prove its charges, the I.R.S. relied upon an analysis of the taxpayer's bank deposits and cash expenditures. Under this method, all deposits to the taxpayer's bank and similar accounts in a single year are added together to determine the gross deposits. An effort is made to identify amounts deposited that are non-taxable, such as gifts, transfers of money between accounts, repayment of loans, and cash that the taxpayer had in his possession prior to that year that was deposited in a bank during that year. This process is called "purification." It results in a figure called net taxable bank deposits.

The I.R.S. agent then adds the amount of expenditures made in cash. For example, in this case, cash the doctor received from fees, he did not deposit, but gave to his wife to buy groceries. The total of this amount and net taxable bank deposits is deemed to equal gross income. This is, in turn, reduced by the applicable deductions and exemptions. The figure arrived at is considered to be "corrected taxable income." It is then compared with the taxable income reported by the taxpayer on his return.

There is always the possibility that the taxpayer deposited cash that he received from a non-taxable source or from income taxed in a prior year but kept on hand as cash or even from unreported income from a prior year kept on hand as cash. Such events are common human occurrences, and this possibility may of itself create reasonable doubt. Therefore, the government must establish in some fashion the amount of cash the taxpayer had on hand at the start of the period. This is part of the government's duty to negate the possibility that bank deposits or cash expenditures in the year under investigation originated from non-taxable sources.

In this court decision, Dr. Loophole lost. His consolation prize was free room and board in a federal penitentiary.

Of course, some taxpayers have tried to avoid taxes by dealing in cash (i.e., eliminating any checks which can be obtained from a bank by an I.R.S. agent). However, an agent may use a net worth method to determine a taxpayer's unreported income. Basically, an agent determines the cost basis of the assets of a taxpayer at the beginning and end of each year under investigation. Total liabilities are deducted from the total assets so that the increase or decrease in net worth over the period of years is determined. To the resulting increase in net worth are added all non-deductible items (i.e., living expenses), then subtract all non-taxable sources of funds to obtain the "true" taxable income to be compared to the reported net income in order to determine any unreported income.

In conclusion, although it is possible to hide taxable income from the I.R.S. the government does have many ingenious ways to catch a dishonest taxpayer. The best strategy is to use all possible tax minimization techniques to reduce your tax liability. But tax evasion is not a legal tax minimization technique.

CHAPTER 3

Hobbyist, Investor, or Dealer

This book is about taxes and antiques. Since almost everyone pays taxes and almost everyone reading these words buys antiques, the authors think you should know how the Internal Revenue Service views the activities.

The I.R.S. conveniently divides everything into two categories: activities pursued with a profit motive and activities pursued with any other motive. The tax laws concerning these two categories differ in one major (and millions of minor) detail. If one pursues an activity with a profit motive and fails not only to make money but also loses money, then the government will share part of that loss by giving the person part of the loss back at tax time. If one pursues an activity with any other motive, then the government will not cover any of the loss.

On the other hand, if a profit is made no matter what the motive, the government wants part of the profit.

Since the purpose of the I.R.S. is to collect as much money as is legally possible, the I.R.S. will try to place as many activities in the non-profit category as possible since more taxes will be collected.

So the first question that must be answered is what is the

motive behind your buying antiques. If the motive is profit, then this book will help you keep as much as possible of the profit. If the motive is other than profit, then this book is also of tremendous value. The sections on recordkeeping, estate planning, auctions, philanthropic activities, and controversies with the I.R.S. are important no matter what your antique buying objectives are.

You fit within one of three major tax categories: hobbyist, investor, or dealer. As the three circles in the chart below depict, you may fall within one, two, or all three tax categories. But overall, the available facts will place you in one category. Your tax treatment depends upon your tax category.

The next section is addressed to the hobbyist since probably the largest number of readers will fall into this category. However, the non-hobbyist should read it carefully because it is all right for

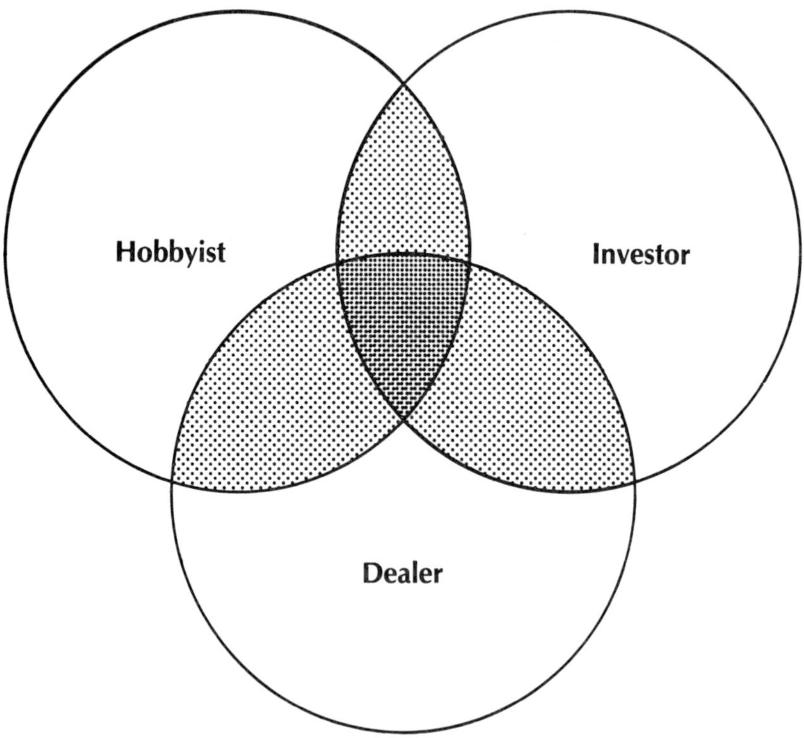

Should your investment monies have been placed in a 1929 Model A Ford Phaeton? The approximate appreciation rate per year from 1970 through 1980 was 16% for a good specimen. Remember—if you were to do this and you are a collector or investor, any appreciation would be taxed at favorable capital gain rates of 40% of your tax bracket. (Photo courtesy of Old Cars Price Guide *magazine, Iola, Wisconsin)*

a hobbyist to act like a businessman, but it is fatal for a businessman to act like a hobbyist.

The Hobbyist

How valuable is this book to someone who completely enjoys the beauty and uniqueness of a beautiful antique and who may even be offended by the idea of selling such beauty for profit? The answer is that there are three stages in the ownership of an antique—acquisition, use, and disposal. Although this book cannot help with the use of a fine piece, it can help with the acquisition and disposal. The section on auctions is useful to anyone interested in antiques, and the section on altered antiques is quite beneficial. The disposal of antiques is also an important part of owning them. Whether the antique is passed on as a gift, willed in an estate, traded for a more valuable piece, or sold outright, there are important tax consequences of each of them.

The first point that should be made is that no matter how an antique is acquired, a careful and complete record should be kept.

For example, a gentleman bought over several years many Cuna Indian artifacts in his travels in South America but kept no records. When he decided to sell the collection to a museum, he was amazed to find that it was worth over thirty thousand dollars. But he did not know his tax basis in the artifacts. An I.R.S. agent might maintain that his basis is zero, and force him to pay taxes on the entire $30,000. What can this taxpayer do? A little knowledge beforehand could have saved this gentleman much time, money, and worry.

What is a hobbyist? Simply put, a hobbyist is an individual who acquires antiques strictly as a hobby. The profit motive has no bearing on what he collects. He collects antiques solely for pleasure. Pleasure rather than "making a profit" is the goal of a hobbyist.

If a hobbyist sells an antique, any gain is considered to be a capital gain. If the item is held for at least twelve months and one day, any gain will be taxed as a long-term capital gain. If the antique is held twelve months or less, any gain is a short-term capital gain. Keep in mind that a long-term capital gain receives favorable tax treatment. Only 40% of a long-term capital gain is taxed. Thus, a long-term capital gain is taxed at 40% of your overall tax bracket plus any appropriate state income tax.

In general, any expenditures incurred by a hobbyist are not deductible, unless they fall into a category that is normally deductible (i.e., interest expense, casualty loss). However, any expenditures may be offset against any hobby gains incurred during the year. For example, if you incur hobbyist expenses of $1,200 during 1981 and have no hobby gain, none of the expenses would be deductible. However, if you incur a $200 hobbyist gain during 1981, $200 of these expenses may be taken as an itemized deduction.

Investor

This section is for the growing number of individuals who have realized that antiques are an excellent investment. Since an investor by definition is trying to make money, this section allows you to keep as much as possible of the profit. As mentioned earlier, a profit motive is viewed favorably by the government, so the major thrust of this section helps to differentiate between a hobbyist and an investor.

The I.R.S. has published some guidelines to determine whether an activity has the dominant objective of a profit:

1. Whether or not the activity is conducted in a business-like manner.
2. The personal expertise of the taxpayer or his advisor.
3. The time and effort expended.
4. The expectation of asset appreciation.
5. Whether or not the taxpayer is successful in other activities.
6. Whether such activity has a history of profit or loss.
7. The taxpayer's financial status.
8. The personal pleasure or recreational aspects of the activity.

Number 8 could be the most troublesome, especially for the investor in small collectibles such as Hummels, coins, or stamps. The I.R.S. is saying that if pleasure is involved, then it may indicate that the activity is a hobby rather than a business or investment activity. However, the courts have stated that "a business will not be turned into a hobby merely because the owner finds it pleasurable; suffering has never been a prerequisite to deductibility."

Hummel figurines might be considered "instant collectibles," as they are still being made today. The original sale prices of some of these were in the $3 to $5 range; today certain of the older ones can easily fetch anywhere from $60 to $300. (Photo courtesy of Mapes Auctioneers/Appraisers, Vestal, New York)

Number 6 has been formalized in the 2-out-of-5 years rule which states that an activity must show a net income in any two out of five consecutive years. However, this 2-out-of-5 years rule is a rebuttable presumption; that is, the I.R.S. can still challenge the deductibility of your losses even if you make a profit 2 out of 5 years.

To aid you in convincing the I.R.S. here are some suggestions to improve your chances of being considered an investor instead of a hobbyist:

1. Maintain a business-like attitude in all antique transactions.
2. Emphasize the investment potential of owning antiques and not the pleasant aspects.

3. Since some antiques are personal and others are for investment, keep such transactions separate even to the extent of setting up a separate checking account.
4. All transactions must be recorded and the records preserved.
5. Ask your antique dealer contacts to make investment suggestions and note their suggestions.
6. Do not attempt to deduct any literature that emphasizes the hobby aspects of antiques. Order and deduct those publications that are investment oriented (such as this book).
7. Do not use an investment property as a personal piece of property. In other words, do not display a fine antique (bought as an investment) in your home.
8. The greater one's wealth, the harder it will be to prove that profit and not pleasure is the primary goal of antique investing.
9. If all else fails and you are classified as a hobbyist, then sell enough of your collection each year to pay your maintenance expenses.

Once the profit motive is firmly established, one must next decide if he is an investor or a dealer. Again, there are significant tax consequences either way.

The line between dealer and investor is somewhat cloudy. After all, both buy and sell antiques and hope to make a profit. However, the I.R.S. views them quite differently both in respect to rate of taxation of profits and the deductibility of losses.

The major difference is that an investor is eligible for capital gains treatment, but a dealer is not. The net result is that an investor can hold an antique for 12 months and one day, sell the antique, and pay taxes on only 40% of the profit. But a dealer cannot obtain this treatment on his inventory.

Another difference is that a dealer can carry back and carry over any net operating losses, but the investor's deductions are often limited to the current year. Further, a dealer does not have to pay a sales tax on purchases, but the dealer must collect the sales tax from the buyer and remit to the appropriate government unit.

However, the tax laws do not define an investor or a dealer (except for securities), so we must look for the distinction in court decisions.

One variable is the expectation of the taxpayer. A dealer is defined as one who buys with the expectation of selling at a profit (not because of an increase in value) that represents his payment as a middleman in performing the services of retailer or wholesaler. An investor buys with the expectation that the antique will increase in value and the profit will result from this increase or appreciation.

The intent of a taxpayer is important. For example, a dealer files a Schedule C but an investor does not.

Another factor is how often buying and selling occurs and the extent of these activities. An investor may sell only once a year, but a dealer will sell weekly or daily. Also, a dealer has no reason to hold an item any longer than necessary, but an investor has a good reason to hold it at least 12 months and one day. So if one bought a rolltop desk and immediately began to advertise it for sale, the seller probably would be classified as a dealer.

Some other criteria might include:

1. The effort and time spent by the taxpayer in buying or selling antiques.
2. Regular professional, promotional or business assistance.
3. The type and quantity of advertising.
4. The overall business nature of the operation.

Unfortunately, there are no clear rules to differentiate an investor from a dealer. The primary point is that one must act in a manner consistent with one's overall goals. You can avoid tax problems by acting in such a manner that your intentions are accurately reflected. The chart below does summarize the major tax results of each category. In general, the investor is in the most favored category.

There are several major ways of identifying antique inventory items for valuation purposes. A small dealer may wish to use the

Your Tax Classification	How Gain is Taxed	Deductibility of Expenses	Payment of Sales Tax
Collector	Capital Gain	Only against any income, D from AGI	Yes
Investor	Capital Gain	D from AGI	Yes
Dealer	Ordinary Income	Ordinary Deduction	No*

*But dealer must collect the sales tax from the buyer and remit to the state. A collector or investor could avoid the sales tax on small collectibles by buying them out of state by mail order, but some states have "USE TAX" statutes and it might be well to check on this with your state tax authorities.

specific identification approach under which the specific item in the antique inventory at the end of the year is matched with the specific purchase invoice. However, for an antique business of any size the inventory items become so intermingled that it is often impossible to use the specific identification approach.

A dealer might use the first-in, first-out approach, which means that the latest antique purchases remain on hand as part of ending inventory. The use of this FIFO method is beneficial during a period of declining prices (a deflationary period) since it reduces taxable income and, therefore, reduces your tax liability.

Another approach is the last-in, first-out technique. The converse of the FIFO approach, this LIFO approach assumes that the most recent antique purchases are sold first and the earliest purchases remain on hand. During periods of rising prices, the LIFO approach is preferred for tax purposes since the cost of goods sold is higher, taxable income is lower, and the overall tax liability is less.

If you believe there will be a continued uptrend in the cost of your inventory, you may wish to switch to the LIFO method.

Fluctuations in earnings are kept at a minimum under the LIFO approach, and this may be helpful from the point of view of satisfying shareholders' demands for dividends and negotiating with labor unions. But once you switch to the LIFO inventory method, you may not change to another method except with the approval of the Commissioner of the I.R.S. Likewise, if you use the LIFO approach for tax purposes, you must also use this same method for financial statement purposes.

The more realistic methods for a dealer to value his inventory are the conventional retail method or the LIFO retail method. Under this conventional retail method, antiques in inventory are valued at the retail selling price. This amount is then reduced to approximate cost with the use of ratios. A separate ratio must be determined for each class of goods or each department. For example, suppose the cost-to-retail ratio is 80% and the retail selling price of the closing inventory is $150,000. Multiplying the closing inventory by 80% produces an inventory cost of $120,000.

The LIFO retail method is essentially a combination of the retail method and the LIFO method. Although not discussed here due to complexity, this method is based upon a layering system.

One final comment is appropriate. Since an antique dealer is required to inventory unsold merchandise on hand at the beginning and end of each year, he is required to use the accrual method of accounting for purchases and sales. The cash method of accounting may not be used for these two items.

CHAPTER 4

Recordkeeping

Many taxpayers fail to appreciate the importance of maintaining and retaining adequate tax records. The tax laws require all taxpayers to keep such records as the I.R.S. Commissioner may prescribe and the willful failure to comply therewith constitutes a misdemeanor. The penalty is a fine of not more than $10,000 or imprisonment for not more than one year, or both, together with the costs of prosecution. Aside from these criminal penalties, the failure to maintain proper records may subject taxpayers to a 5% negligence penalty.

A taxpayer must maintain such records as will enable him to file a tax return which clearly reflects his taxable income. To clearly reflect income, his income must be indicated with as much accuracy as standard methods of accounting permit. Cases are legion in which a decision went against a taxpayer either at the I.R.S. level or in court because his records were inadequate. Remember, in most situations the burden of proof is upon the taxpayer to show that any alleged deficiency is incorrect. That is, supporting records may be needed to prove the correctness of items of income or deductions when challenged by an I.R.S. agent. Suggestion: Set aside a particular drawer which can be used to accumulate applicable tax records such as invoices or receipts during the year.

Record charts for antiques may be purchased or made (see below). On such charts, including the date and description of each purchase can be quite important. Where the same type of collectible is purchased at different times and you have no way of specific identification, the I.R.S. may use the so-called first-in, first-out rule (FIFO). Under this rule the antiques sold are deemed to be the earliest items acquired. Because of differences in holding periods and tax bases, a sale of an antique may result in either a short-term or long-term gain or loss, depending upon which collectible is considered sold first. By maintaining adequate records an investor is able to control the type and amount of gain or loss to be recognized when he sells a portion of his position in a type of antique (i.e., similar plates).

In order for a taxpayer to take advantage of favorable features of the tax laws (accrual method, installment method, etc.), adequate books and records must be maintained. In a recent court case a taxpayer was not allowed to use a special method because his books and records were inadequate. If a taxpayer keeps only such records as to permit the taxpayer to determine his income on a cash method of accounting, he can not complain if the I.R.S. determines his income under the cash method. "Where no systematic records and bookkeeping practices are employed, use of the accrual method of accounting is not allowed the taxpayer . . . and the taxpayer is presumed to be on the cash method of accounting."

The type of records that should be maintained by an investor is not specified in the law. Such records need not be elaborate or formal. Simple records should encourage you to make the entries promptly as income items are received and payments for any deductible expenses are made. Sales slips, bills, invoices, receipts, canceled checks, and other documents are often sufficient evidence to support deductions claimed on your tax return. Dates of sales and purchases of antiques are very important due to the importance of the long-term and short-term classification.

At the very minimum, records should be maintained for at least four years after the due date of the tax return or the date the tax is paid, whichever is less. Due to the importance of the income averaging rules, records should probably be kept from six to ten years. Returns of prior years can greatly simplify making out a current return. In fact, as long as you keep a collectible, you should keep any applicable information concerning such item. Treat your purchases and sales just as you would treat other investments such as stocks or real estate. A business-like attitude is very important with respect to any hobby-related investments. For more information, write for a copy of *Guide to Record Retention Requirements,* G.P.O., Washington, DC 20402, $2.00.

Expenses are deductible under two major areas of the tax law. First, all ordinary or necessary expenditures paid or incurred during a tax year in carrying on any trade or business (for example, an antique dealer) are allowable as business deductions. Such allowable business deductions include such items as salaries, travel and entertainment expense, advertising expenditures, depreciation or rent of an antique shop, supplies, insurance, utilities, and so forth. Obviously, expenses incurred to attend an antique convention to purchase collectibles should be deductible by a dealer. Second, any ordinary or necessary expenditures paid or incurred during a tax year are deductible if they are made (a) for the production or collection of income, or (b) for the management, conservation, or maintenance of property (i.e., antiques) held for the production of income. An investor falls into this latter category.

A collector probably does not fall within either of these categories since a taxpayer may not deduct the expenses of maintaining his investment property if such property is held "primarily as a sport, hobby, or recreation." As a general rule a collector's expenses are deductible only to the extent of any hobby income (e.g., gain on sale of antiques), unless the expenses fall into a category which is normally deductible (e.g., interest expense, sales taxes, or casualty losses).

Deductible expenses incurred by an individual in connection

ANTIQUE GAIN (OR LOSS) RECORD

Item	Purchase		Sale		Gain (or Loss)	Comment
	Date	Amount	Date	Amount		
Silver Tea Set	1/27/55	250.00	6/19/79	750.00	500.00	sold to: D. J. Haskins
29 "A" Ford	3/61	875.00	5/80	3500.00	2625.00	sold to: Frank Burnes
Bisque Doll	3/67	27.50	5/80	900.00	872.50	sold at Auction
Beer Can Collection	3/73	100.00	5/80	75.00	(25.00)	sold at Loss
Regina Music Box	8/74	850.00	7/81	1850.00	1000	sold at Convention

ANTIQUE EXPENSE RECORD*

Date	Expense	Comment
8/15/81	$ 3.85	telephone to Chicago for player piano parts
8/17/81	$ 4.80	can of stain for Steinway refinishing
8/17/81	$ 14.00	replacement piano caster
8/17/81	$ 2.60	shipping charges on parts

*Be sure to keep receipts, invoices, etc., so you will be able to prove that you incurred the expense.

with antiques and other investments include those paid for custodian services for the collection of income, safekeeping, and the delivery and receipt of antiques acquired or disposed of, investment advice, including financial publications and books, compensation for secretaries, bookkeepers, and other office employees, office rent, safe deposit box rentals, accounting and auditing services. Beware: the I.R.S. has said that the expenses of an investor in attending stockholders' meetings of corporations in which he owns stock are ordinarily non-deductible personal expenditures because they are not ordinary and necessary expenses incurred for the production of income.

Traveling expenses incurred while away from home (such as travel fares, meals, and lodging) are deductible. But for each expenditure the taxpayer must maintain data or a diary substantiating:

1. The amount.
2. The time and place of travel or entertainment.
3. The business purpose.
4. The business relationship to the taxpayer of each person entertained.

In addition, a receipt must be obtained where practicable for any expenditure for lodging while away from home and for any other expenditure of $50 or more. In lieu of accounting for the actual amount spent, certain reasonable per diem allowances for travel away from home and mileage allowances may be deducted if all the other substantiation requirements are met (for example, time and place of travel). If the documentation and business purposes are not within the prescribed requirements of the law, it is possible under certain circumstances not only that the business will be denied a deduction, but also that the recipient, even if only in an employee's status, will be deemed to have taxable income in the amount of any reimbursement he receives.

Dues paid to organizations directly related to a taxpayer's trade or business are deductible as ordinary and necessary expenses.

Thus, dues paid to antique organizations may be deductible by a dealer or investor.

Most advisors recommend to taxpayers that they should take a deduction for safe deposit box rental. Apparently, the I.R.S. is beginning to look closely at this deduction even though the deduction may be only $10–30. You must ask yourself: Is it worth an audit to claim a small deduction? This small deduction may target an audit whereby the auditing agent finds a much larger questionable item.

The I.R.S. may also be looking at this deduction in order to find "hidden" income. If audited, you'll have to declare what investment items are in the box in order to obtain the deduction. Obviously, if the collectibles or other investment items (which you declare) "disappear" in the future without appearing on the tax return, the I.R.S. will know that you are not reporting these transactions.

You should be aware that when a boxholder dies, the bank tags the box so that a survivor cannot empty the box. Bank employees read the daily newspapers and monitor the death lists in order to determine when to inventory the contents and seal the box. Bank employees then send the inventory list to the appropriate state official. Once the box is sealed, a court order is required to open it.

It may be possible to avoid having your box sealed at death by setting up the box in the name of a business, with two or more officers listed (i.e., husband and wife).

Generally, only the executor of the estate is allowed access to the box. Thus, each of us should have a will with a designated executor. If there is no will or executor, the bank will probably send the contents of the box directly to the probate court. Thus, it is wise to have a copy of your will, burial specifications, and an inventory of the box outside of the safe deposit box.

In the case of co-owners, remember that you must have a trustworthy co-owner. One of the co-owners can strip the box of any valuables at any time. A co-leasee has the same rights as the

This large doll is German bisque, with a current value of several hundreds of dollars. The small one is a "China Head" of porcelain, which typically sell in the $50–$150 range. Enormous amounts of dollar appreciation have occurred in the doll market, and collectors and dealers are well-advised to keep careful records for Uncle Sam's I.R.S. agents are quite aware of this fact! (Photo courtesy of Mapes Auctioneers/Appraisers, Vestal, New York)

actual owner of the box. You cannot remove a co-owner. You cannot restrict his or her access.

A person can be listed as a deputy of the box. A deputy can be removed from this status at any time.

CHAPTER 5

Business Organizations

There are basically three organizational forms with variations on some of the three. These forms are sole proprietor, partnership, and corporation. Each has advantages and disadvantages so none can be recommended without a consideration of all the facts.

SOLE PROPRIETORSHIP As the name implies, one person owns and operates the business. All of the profits are taxed as ordinary income and the owner has unlimited liability. The owner has limited means of raising additional capital. He is usually limited to savings, loans, or after taxes profits as the sources of capital. This limitation becomes very serious when and if the business wishes to expand.

The advantages are that one is the boss and he answers to no one else, all profits are his, many deductions are available as business expenses, and profits are taxed only once.

PARTNERSHIP Also as the name implies, a partnership is a group gathered together for mutual benefit. In one form of the partnership, a General Partnership, all partners are general partners and the ownership is divided among the partners as is mutually agreed upon. All partners in a general partnership have unlimited liability and, very importantly, participate in the operation and management of the partnership. Also, the basis of a person's interest in the partnership is the money or property he has contributed or the skills he may have contributed (or a combination of both).

To partially correct some of the shortcomings of the General Partnership, a special form called a Limited Partnership was created. This Limited Partnership has two classes—a General Partner and a Limited Partner. The Limited Partner(s) has limited liability and may not be actively involved in the day-to-day operation. The General Partner(s) has unlimited liability and is actively involved in the day-to-day operation. To preserve the protection of limited liability, the Limited Partner must avoid actively participating in the day-to-day operation of the business.

The limited liability referred to above means that a Limited Partner can lose no more than the original investment. If additional liability is created by the operation of the business, then it will all fall on the General Partner(s). In exchange for the protection of the Limited Partner, the General Partner generally demands and deserves a larger portion of the profits than he otherwise would receive.

CORPORATION A corporation is a mechanism for raising capital in a relatively straightforward manner by selling stock. As an added bonus, it also provides liability protection. Other tax and non-tax advantages are:

1. Parts of a corporation or shares are easier to sell than are partnership or proprietorship interests.
2. A corporation is immortal and can survive the deaths of any or all of the stockholders. A partnership, in contrast, cannot survive the death or even withdrawal of one of the partners.
3. Shareholders are in theory unlimited in number, but partners are limited.

4. From a tax point of view, it is safer and easier to split income among members by stock gifts than under any other form of organization.
5. All the fringe benefits that a large corporation uses, such as medical insurance, life insurance, profit-sharing, and pension plans are also available to a small corporation.

A major disadvantage of a corporation is the double taxation—once at the corporate level and again on the dividends at the individual level. The corporate rates are progressive in nature as follows:

Taxable Income	1981	1982	1983, thereafter
$ 0–$ 25,000	17%	16%	15%
$25,000–$ 50,000	20%	19%	18%
$50,000–$ 75,000	30%	30%	30%
$75,000–$100,000	40%	40%	40%
Above $100,000	46%	46%	46%

If you decide to incorporate, be sure your tax advisor issues so-called section 1244 stock. This type of stock will allow you to receive an ordinary deduction (rather than a capital loss) in case your venture is not successful. This technique must be made at incorporation and involves no disadvantages.

As in the case of partnerships, corporations come in two shapes—a regular corporation and a Subchapter S corporation. We discuss the Subchapter S corporation in detail below.

Subchapter S Corporation

For many years the double tax on corporate taxable income has been a significant deterrent to the use of the corporate form of organization by small businesses. A Subchapter S election, however, can relieve this double tax burden on closely-held corporations and their stockholders who elect and qualify to come under these valuable tax provisions.

In order for a corporation and its shareholders to obtain the benefits of Subchapter S, the corporation must meet the following requirements:

1. For years after 1978 and through 1981, the maximum number of stockholders is 15. Thereafter, a Subchapter S corporation may have as many as 25 stockholders.
2. All shareholders must be individuals or estates. However, grantor trusts and voting trusts are permitted. Further, a testamentary trust can be a shareholder, but only for 60 days after shares are transferred to it. A trust is a valid stockholder after 1981 if its sole income beneficiary is a disabled individual who is a resident or citizen of the U.S.
3. It must have only one class of issued stock. Authorized but unissued stock, such as preferred, is disregarded.
4. No shareholder can be a non-resident alien.
5. It must not own 80 percent or more of the stock of any affiliated corporation that has begun business activities or had taxable income.

In addition to the stock and shareholder requirements above, in order for a Subchapter S corporation to remain qualified, it must meet the following requirements:

1. The corporation must not derive more than 80 percent of its gross receipts from sources outside the United States.
2. Other than during the first two years of its active existence, the corporation cannot receive passive investment income in any year amounting to more than 20 percent of its gross receipts, or in excess of $3,000.

The term "passive investment income" means gross receipts derived from royalties, rents, dividends, interest, annuities, and gains from the sale or exchange of stock or securities (but not antiques).

If a corporation meets the requirements above, if it files a proper election, and if the shareholders unanimously consent, the corporation and its shareholders will be taxed under Subchapter S. The election and consents must be filed with the local District Director during either (1) the first 75 days of the taxable year for which this special status is desired, or (2) any time during the preceding year. Once made, the election remains in effect for all subsequent years unless (1) revoked by the shareholders, (2) the corporation ceases to qualify, or (3) a new person becomes a shareholder and affirmatively refuses to consent to the election within 60 days after he acquires his stock interest.

Since a Subchapter S corporation is essentially a tax-reporting rather than taxpaying entity (except for a capital gain greater than $25,000), its income is taxed to its shareholders regardless of whether it has been distributed. Stock ownership at the end of the tax year is the criterion for allocating the constructive dividend among shareholders. Such income is assigned to the stockholders of record on the last day of the corporate year in proportion to their stock ownership. Changes in ownership during the tax year are ignored. Hence, a bona fide shift of ownership near the close of the tax year can be a tax-saving device whenever income can be shifted to taxpayers in lower tax brackets.

Losses are allocated to present and prior shareholders on a daily basis. Thus, length of ownership affects allocations of losses. Any net operating loss of a Subchapter S corporation is passed through and deducted as a business loss by the shareholders in determining their respective amounts of gross income. If the loss exceeds a shareholder's other income for the year, a net operating loss for him is created, which he may carry back for three years and carry forward for seven years under the general rules for net operating losses (15-year carryover for corporations).

Compared to doing business as a proprietor or through a partnership, a small businessman has available to him the following benefits of Subchapter S status:

1. The corporate tax is avoided (except for large capital gains).
2. The legal benefit of conducting business in corporate form so as not to be personally liable for corporate debts.
3. The tax benefit of being able to deduct his share of a corporate net operating loss to the extent of his investment in stock and debt receivables of the corporation.
4. Group life insurance.
5. Non-taxable employee accident and health benefit reimbursements.
6. Timing of income taxation to the shareholders if the corporation can use a fiscal year.

If you are currently operating your antique business as a proprietor or through a partnership, you should consider incorporating your business and electing Subchapter S. Likewise, if you are currently operating as a regular corporation, you should consider the advantages of electing Subchapter S status. For more detail, see *Organizing, Operating, and Terminating Subchapter S Corporations* ($29.50, Information Services, P.O. Box 9027, College Station, TX 77840).

An example will show the real difference between these various business forms. Suppose three individuals have $5,000 each to invest in an antique business. Individual A is a part-time dealer and B and C are more or less involved in antiques. There are five options open to them. These options are shown in Table. I

In the sole proprietorship, B and C loan A $5,000 each and A will pay 10% interest with the business as the only collateral for the loan.

In the partnership, Limited or General, A, B, and C will own 1/3 interest in the business and pay $5,000 each.

In the corporation, Subchapter S or regular, A, B, and C will own 1/3 of the shares of the corporation.

In any business three things can happen, win, lose, or draw.

Table I shows what will happen in two situations. In Section I, the business makes $15,000 profit, and in Section II the business loses all its capital and incurs an additional obligation of $15,000.

Table I
Profit and Loss Under Different Structure

Section I—$15,000 profit

Business form

	Proprietor	Partnership		Corporation	
Individual		Regular	Limited*	Regular	Sub S
A	14,000	5,000	5,000	4,000	5,000
B	500	5,000	5,000	4,000	5,000
C	500	5,000	5,000	4,000	5,000

Section II—$30,000 loss

	Proprietor	Partnership		Corporation	
Individual		Regular	Limited*	Regular	Sub S
A	(20,000)	(10,000)	(20,000)	(5,000)	(10,000)
B	(5,000)	(10,000)	(5,000)	(5,000)	(10,000)
C	(5,000)	(10,000)	(5,000)	(5,000)	(10,000)

*In the limited partnership A is the General Partner and B and C are Limited Partners.

If the business is successful, then there are few differences between the Regular Partnership, Limited Partnership, and Subchapter S corporation. All profits must be shown and are taxable—even if they are not distributed. Only the Regular corporation can escape taxation at the individual level by not distributing the profit.

In Section I, one notes a significant difference between the Regular and Subchapter S corporation in terms of the profit. The Regular corporation is taxed at the corporate level and at the individual level when and if dividends are declared. The Subchapter S corporation is taxed only at the individual level, but all proceeds are taxable immediately.

If the business goes bad and loses the original $15,000 and $15,000 more, then important differences show up. The sole proprietor will be held responsible to pay the losses. In the Regular Partnership everybody is held responsible for the loss and everybody must pay extra. However, in the Limited Partnership only the General Partner is held liable for the loss in excess of the original $5,000 investment.

On the corporate form side in the Subchapter S situation, no one can make the individual pay more than his original investment, but the stockholder can deduct the corporate losses directly on his individual tax return (Form 1040) to the extent of any stock or loan basis.

In the Regular corporation, if the stock becomes worthless, then no one can make the individual pay more, but only the original investment can be written off as a loss.

If, in Section I, everybody agreed to take out the money due them, pay taxes on it (50% bracket) and return the rest to the business for future growth, then out of the original $30,000, there would be $22,500 in each option except Regular corporation where there would be $27,000 available—a twenty percent increase over the other four options. The taxes on this twenty percent or $4,500 is deferred until later and acts as an interest-free loan. In essence the government comes in as an almost equal partner ($5,000 versus $4,500) in promoting the growth of your business.

In summary, if one wants immediate cash, then four options are available, but if one wants to let the business grow without cash withdrawal, then the Regular corporation may be best.

One method of converting dividends into capital gains is to allow dividends to accumulate within the corporation and then later sell the stock. A corporation can accumulate at least $150,000 ($250,000 after 1981) without getting into trouble. Also, capital gain may be obtained by accumulating the earnings and later liquidating the company. Finally, the income tax at the individual

Roller organs, such as this "Concert" model made by the Autophone Company of Ithaca, New York, around the turn of the century, were available for less than $50 as recently as 1955. As this book is written, a nice one will easily bring ten times, that, a 1,000% increase in value. (Dan Adams photo, courtesy of Q. David Bowers)

level may be avoided by dying with the stock and allowing your heirs to receive a step-up in tax basis.

There are no reasons to stop a corporation from investing excess corporate funds in hard assets such as antiques. Do not use these assets as personal assets, however. Put them in a safe deposit box and let them appreciate.

Or purchase antique furniture or prints to be used in the business. Nineteenth-century music boxes, miniatures, and eighteenth century dolls could be placed in a locked glass display in a reception room. A public relations firm which has a number of politicians as clients could easily assemble a political campaign button display. Use your imagination. The Exchange Bank of

Chicago, Illinois has a permanent collection of both old and contemporary photographs.

Of course, the profit, when sold, would be corporate income and there would be a corporate tax, unless a Subchapter S election is made. A Subchapter S election would avoid the corporate tax and allow the gains to be taxed only at the stockholder level.

CHAPTER 6

Buying

There are basically three sources of antiques—private individuals, auctions, and dealers. The price paid will usually increase as one goes up the scale. Also, the reliability of the information concerning the sales item increases as one goes up the scale.

A very simple rule to follow in any antique transaction is to get it in writing. If any verifiable statement is made concerning an item, ask that such information be included on the sales receipt. If for no other reason than good bookkeeping, a complete description including price and date should be kept on each item purchased. Before you pay several hundred dollars for a rare 1930 movie poster, get it in writing. Be sure of yourself before you pay $5,000 for a nineteenth-century doll.

Pricing Strategy

As is discussed later in the chapter on auctions, one must always be aware of who is buying and for what purpose.

The dealer can only pay about 50% of the retail price and make a profit. An investor can pay about 70% of the selling price

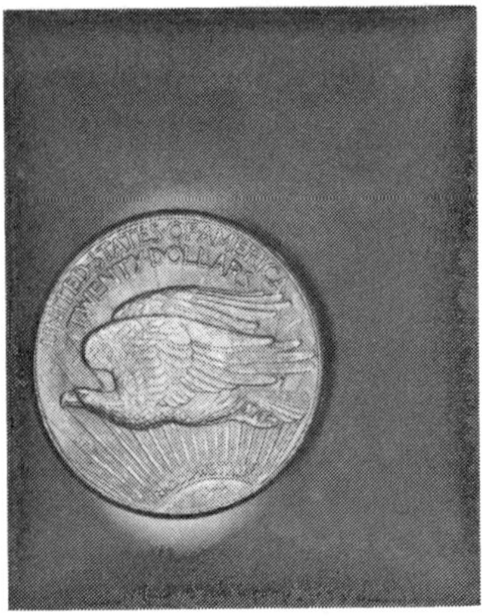

The condition of a collectible has an important impact on value. This 1924S Double Eagle $20 gold coin had a retail price of $2,000 in MS-60 condition in the 1981 "Red Book." The same coin in VF-20 condition was listed at $850. Almost three million of these coins were minted in the old San Francisco mint. Buyers beware! (Photos courtesy of Bowers & Ruddy Galleries, Los Angeles, California)

(not necessarily the retail price) to make an adequate return on his money. The hobbyist can and will often pay retail price in order to get just the piece he or she wants.

Also, the price of an item will vary significantly depending upon the location of the item. If one wants good seventeenth-century English furniture, the cheapest place is England, not New York City.

Appraisals

Antiques are usually intensely individualistic items—truly one of a kind. Exceptions are newer items, some quite valuable, such as stamps, coins, and cars. These items are exceptions also in that information is readily available on the cost of these items.

However, for most items, the question of how much is it worth is very difficult to answer. But for insurance purposes, estate purposes, contribution purposes, and investment purposes some value must be attached to the item. The value most often attached is the retail value of the item—the price a willing buyer will pay a willing seller.

Most antique dealers will evaluate your antiques for a rather modest fee. However, if you are unsure of the approximate value and you are considering selling the items, never tell the appraiser this fact because he may undervalue them in hopes of purchasing them himself.

Three Golden Profitability Rules

1. Buy like a dealer.
2. Think like a hobbyist.
3. Keep records like an investor.

Rule 1: Buy antiques like a dealer. Buy as close to wholesale as possible. Bargain! Do not pay too much for an item just because you want it. The profit is in the purchase.

Rule 2: Think like a hobbyist. Try to look ahead into the future. Will a hobbyist in the future wish to purchase the antique you are about to purchase? Avoid fads. Buy those antiques which have shown a steady increase in value for many years.

Rule 3: Keep records like an investor. By keeping proper records, less of your profit will receive the warm embrace of the friendly tax collectors (federal, state, and local revenuers). The best type of income is in taxed-saved dollars—they're not taxable.

CHAPTER 7

Auctions

An auction is a transaction between a buyer and a seller carried out by an agent called an auctioneer. The purpose of this transaction is to get the highest possible price for the item. To be successful at auction, one must examine and understand the purpose of each element involved—auction, auctioneer, buyer, and seller.

AUCTION The mechanics of auctions are fairly simple. The auctioneer secures enough material to have a sale and then gets enough interested buyers together and proceeds to sell the merchandise. The owner of the merchandise will determine if the auction is an *absolute* auction or a *reserve* auction. An absolute auction has no minimum selling price and the top dollar takes the merchandise. A reserve auction has a minimum acceptable *final* price or the item may be withdrawn. A further word on reserve auctions: the starting bidding may be lower than the acceptable bid and the auctioneer hopes to get the bidding up over the minimum.

AUCTIONEER The auctioneer is the agent of the seller and must try to get the highest price for the merchandise offered. He does not like to withdraw items in a reserve auction. If there is no sale, there is no commission for the auctioneer. This fact prevents the auctioneer from accepting items he knows he can not sell at a reasonable price. The function of the auctioneer is to create a spirit of competition between the various buyers that will drive the price higher. An illegal manuever used by disreputable auctioneers is a "bye" bidder. A bidder will bid only to drive the price up without any intention of buying. If the "bye" bidder accidentally buys the item, then the item is merely returned to inventory and will be resold at a later auction. It is fairly easy to spot a rigged auction by waiting until after the auction and noticing if some of the material was not picked up. Also, if the same item is sold more than once on different occasions, then the auction may be rigged.

BUYER A buyer's role in the auction is to buy at the lowest possible price. To accomplish this feat, there are several firm rules to follow. These rules are summarized, and then the rationale given.

1. Always personally examine every item on which you expect to bid.
2. Set an absolute maximum you are willing to pay for an item, and then stick to it.
3. Come early and stay late.
4. Don't be the first to bid on an item.
5. Don't hurry the bidding.
6. Try to determine who is your competition.
7. The profit is in the purchase.
8. Enjoy the auction. If you don't buy today, there is always tomorrow.

Rule 1: Always examine. Obviously one should look at what you are buying. If you are uncertain and the antique is expensive, then the price of an expert opinion is well worthwhile. Even if you have no intention of buying, the acquired ability to dis-

Collectibles can run into money. One 1787 gold Doubloon, punch on wing, sold in the 1979 Garrett sale for $725,000. In the same year in "Auction 1979 sale," a 1787 Doubloon went for a mere $430,000. (Photo courtesy of Bowers & Ruddy Galleries, Los Angeles, California)

tinguish between English oak and American oak or seventeenth-century dovetailing and eighteenth-century dovetailing will be invaluable.

Rule 2: Always set a limit on an item and then don't exceed it. If there is a very nice walnut rolltop desk you think is worth $2,500 retail and you are an investor interested in a 30 percent return, then you cannot pay more than 70% of retail or 0.7 x $2,500 = $1,750.00. By imposing a limit you assure yourself a good buy if you get it and you hold down the general price level if someone else gets it.

Rule 3: Come early and stay late. Any auction consists of fair, good, and fine materials. An auctioneer will usually show some of the fine items first in order to raise the general price level, and introduce the good or fair stuff in the middle. He holds the rest of the fine items until the end in order to hold his audience. Frequently, if you must leave early, you can "bribe" the auctioneer into bringing up a fine piece earlier by guaranteeing a high opening bid.

Rule 4: Don't be the first to bid on an item and never accept the auctioneer's first asking. If the desk mentioned above is presented and the auctioneer asks for a bid of $1,500, don't let him tell you what to do. Refuse to bid. One of two things will happen. Either he gets his bid of $1,500 or after a suitable effort the auctioneer will lower the starting bid to $1,200. If the auctioneer refuses to lower the opening bid, you may feel free to put in a lower bid yourself. There is nothing magic about his first asking price. Get the auctioneer's attention and say $1,200.

If some "spoil sport" accepts his opening bid of $1,500, then pause until the last possible second before entering your bid. This tactic makes the original bidder wonder if he has made a mistake because nobody else is bidding. After the auctioneer has asked for $1,600 a few times, then bid $1,550. This halving of the increase may have two effects. One is to give you more room and the other guy more chance to worry and possibly quit. At $100 a bid, only three bids are needed to go over your limit and one of them must be yours. At $50 a bid, six bids are needed to go over your limit. The other effect is more subtle. It conveys to everyone the impression that you really are not all that impressed with the desk and maybe they should not be either.

An alternate but sometimes highly effective tactic is to overbid the auctioneer. The auctioneer will frequently say that it is only $50 more. Well, if three people are bidding, the "only $50" becomes only "$150 more per round. If the bidding is going $1,200, 1,250, 1,300, 1,350, 1,400, 1,450, 1,500, etc., you can see that your limit is fast approaching so jump straight to your limit of $1,750.

Now it has suddenly become $250 more instead of "only $50 more." This tactic may break the spell and make people think a little before they go on up.

Rule 5: It is always to the benefit of the auctioneer to have bidding carried on at a frenzied pace. Therefore it is to your advantage if you can hesitate a bit before entering your bid, just to get the whole affair operating a little more slowly.

Rule 6: Evaluate your competition. There are basically three types of buyers at an auction. Arranged in order from most competitive to least (i.e., paying the most to paying the least) are the collector, the investor, and the dealer. The dealer can only pay about 50% of retail. An investor pays from 60% to 75% of retail. The proverbial little old lady in tennis shoes will pay retail or above if she (or he) really, really wants that cut glass bon bon dish. If, in our desk example, everybody in the house will bid

$1,200 but the competition thins significantly at $1,400 and only one very determined bidder who pauses only long enough to hear you bid and then bids again $1,600—forget it. Let it go. Don't keep the overall price high because it will hurt you later.

Rule 7: The profit is in the purchase. Do not pay too much for antiques. In order to obtain a reasonable profit, you must obtain an antique as close to wholesale as possible.

Rule 8: Enjoy the auction. If you don't buy anything, do not worry—your time will come again. Watch the auctioneer and the audience. It's great entertainment.

SELLER The seller is the individual who stands to lose or gain at an auction. Try to remain objective and recognize that you win some, lose some, and usually draw. Try also to evaluate the performance of all your offering—not any particular piece.

COMMISSION In the seller's section seems an appropriate place to mention that a fee, usually 10%, is paid to the auctioneer. In the past, the seller always paid this cost. However, some of the large auction houses have started charging the *buyer* the commission. Time alone will tell if this change will catch on. Typically for jewelry auctions, there is a 10% commission charged to the buyer and a 10% commission charged to the seller.

CHAPTER 8

Reproductions and Altered Antiques

Every investor, collector, or dealer hopes that he never has to read this chapter, but there are reproductions passed off as originals. Even more cunning are the addition or subtraction pieces in which an old but common (and therefore) inexpensive antique is modified to look like a rare (and therefore) expensive antique. For example, there are French bisque dolls with false identification marks stamped on the back.

The first rule of thumb is always to get a written description from your supplier. No legitimate dealer should hesitate to give you a written statement completely describing the antique purchased. You should always get this description in writing even when you have no doubt of the authenticity in order to have a complete record for your files. Needless to say, if the dealer refuses, find another dealer or be prepared to gamble that you know more than the dealer.

Assume for the sake of discussion, the following occurred. You purchased an oak highboy (circa 1750) from an unreliable dealer for $1,800. When you had it appraised, you found it consisted of a good lowboy (circa 1800) worth $400 and a bureau that had been cut off (valued at $50).

You have a loss of $1,350 and you are faced with the question of what to do and whether or not you can deduct the loss. The tax law provides three basic categories under which losses may be deducted. These are as follows:

1. losses incurred in a trade or business (a dealer),
2. losses incurred in any transaction entered into for profit (an investor), or
3. losses not connected with trade or business which arise from fire, storm, shipwreck, or other casualty, or from theft (a dealer, investor, or collector).

If the taxpayer who bought the altered piece was either a dealer or an investor, his loss is clearly deductible when sold under either of the first two provisions, respectively. But see Chapter 2 which indicates the criteria to distinguish between a hobby or a business. In general, whether or not a transaction was entered into for profit is in fact a question to be established in light of all circumstances. In the case of altered antiques, the deduction should be taken in the year you sell the antique. However, make sure that the buyer is aware of the fact that the antique has been altered—preferably in writing. As for an investor, he may wish to try the casualty loss route below since casualty loss treatment is more beneficial than capital loss treatment.

However, for a taxpayer who is not an investor or a dealer the problem of deductibility is not quite so simple. Recall that gains from transactions on property held for personal use are capital gains but losses are never deductible unless an involuntary conversion is involved. However, counterfeit or altered antiques could possibly be classified as a "worthless" investment purchased on the representation of false and fraudulent sales offers and, therefore, deductible as a theft loss in the year purchased since there is no reasonable prospect of recovery.

The term "theft" is deemed to include, but shall not necessarily be limited to, larceny, embezzlement, and robbery. It is not necessary that the alleged thief be convicted or even prosecuted, as long as a "theft" in fact occurred under the law of the state wherein it was sustained. Thus, it depends upon whether the worthless property is a theft under local law. An essential element of the offense of false pretenses in some states is that the accused individual obtain money with the intent to defraud. This intent to defraud need not be proved by direct evidence, but may be proved by facts and circumstances. Thus, any misrepresentation of a past fact, knowingly and designedly made to induce another to part with his property, is a false pretense under some state laws.

You, the taxpayer, have the burden of proof in an intent to defraud situation. If, however, a "theft" does occur under local law, it would be deductible as a theft loss to the extent of your adjusted basis in the antique, reduced by any reimbursement (none in your case), and also reduced by the $100 non-deductible feature. This $100 non-deductible feature would apply to *each* theft. Therefore, your *possible* deduction would be $1,250 ($1,800 – 400 – 50 – 100), assuming you itemize your deductions. Such deductions would be available only in the year in which the reproduced or altered antiques are discovered.

There is one dark cloud on the horizon with respect to this casualty loss route. In a recent Tax Court case a purchaser of unregistered stock tried to describe the sales pitch of a promoter (e.g., investment huckster) as fraudulent when the taxpayer's investment went sour. The securities under California Blue Sky laws were required to be registered for sale in California. This law is very strict; the seller did not register the securities and therefore committed a crime even though he may have had no criminal intent.

This state statute did not help this taxpayer because the federal tax laws require a taxpayer to show that the person who solicited the funds knowingly made false representations which he intended the taxpayer to rely upon. Here the Tax Court was unimpressed by the actual evidence the taxpayer produced in order to show that misrepresentation occurred. Thus, a written description of the antique along with authenticity is quite important for tax purposes. You must have evidence that the classic features of criminal fraud or misrepresentation existed.

If an investor or collector does not wish to try the casualty loss route with altered or reproduced antiques, you have other options. First, during the year you discover the fake antiques, sell them as altered antiques to a reliable dealer, take your loss, but make sure you have enough long-term (LT) or short-term (ST) capital gains to offset the loss (preferably short-term gains). For example, suppose you sell both for a total of $450. You will have a LTCL of approximately $1,350 which can offset $1,350 of LTCGs from your other transactions. It is, or course, important that you have enough capital gains to cover the loss. Otherwise, the loss will not be allowed if you are merely a collector.

There is another alternative. You could take the antique and group it with another antique (or antiques) which have appreciated by at least $1,350 and trade this batch of antiques to a dealer for other antiques (be sure he knows some of the antiques are altered). In effect, you transfer the basis in the altered antiques over to your new group and eventually when you sell such new antiques the altered antiques basis offsets some of the capital gain. Of course, by trading you postpone the loss into the future.

You may wish to take action against the company which has cheated you. These are some steps you may take:

1. Write the company, telling them you plan to write all the major antique publications telling your story if they do not refund your money within 12 days. Do this writing if they do not refund your money. Send carbon copies of your letters to the antique firm in question.
2. Write the state's Attorney General, the post office, and Federal Trade Commission.
3. Write local and national antique organizations.
4. Some states have Deceptive Trade Practices statutes. A plaintiff can obtain triple damages plus attorneys' fees. These statutes make it easier to prove fraud. Find a lawyer

Mechanical banks have been collectible for many years, and are highly desirable if they have their original paint and are in nice condition. (Photo courtesy of Mapes Auctioneers/Appraisers, Vestal, New York)

who will take your case based upon the amount you win (a percentage).

5. Check to see if your state has a small claims division. Bring suit here since you do not need a lawyer and it is cheaper.

There are small claims courts in the various states. The reason for these small claims courts are to provide individuals with a speedy, informal, and inexpensive means of resolving conflicts of small monetary value.

The monetary ceiling for jurisdiction varies from state to state (e.g., $100 in Iowa, $200 in Texas, $2,000 in New Mexico). In most states you may take your case to court without hiring a lawyer.

Beware, however, even if you win your decision, there is no certainty that you will collect your claim. It is estimated that about one-third of the victorious plaintiffs are unable to collect their claims. Since the collection process is performed by the local sheriff or constable on a fee basis, they often favor the larger clients (i.e., companies, utilities, etc.).

Although these courts do have defects, check out the small claims court in your area. Use it—it is there for all of us.

Collecting and investing in antiques is definitely a case of "buyer beware." Many dealers travel the country, obtaining a temporary hotel or motel room, holding auctions to sell "new" antiques as "old" products. This is especially true for oriental rugs. Poor quality rugs are offered as good quality by painting in faded spots or cutting back undesirable white threads. Machine-made rugs are sold as hand-made rugs. You can never be too careful.

CHAPTER 9

The Effect Antiques Have on Your Estate

In these days of inflation, investments grow in value more rapidly than ever before. Many people are surprised that they have problems with a tax that they have never heard of before—the estate tax. The federal government imposes a tax on the "fair market value" of all assets, less liabilities, held by a person when he dies. This includes life insurance (even though paid to someone else) and property owned jointly with someone else. The first $175,000 of a person's estate who dies in 1981 is not taxable ($350,000 in a community property state).* Thereafter, the tax graduates from 32% up to an eventual 50% in the highest bracket. Many state governments also impose inheritance taxes on the amounts received by the individual heirs. Here again there is usually an exemption for a certain amount of property, depending upon the relationship of the heir to the person who died. However, there are many instances where the federal and state death taxes consumed a major portion of the decedent's estate where

*The law is written so that the first $47,000 of estate taxes is not paid, which converts into a taxable estate of about $175,000. These figures are increasing each year beginning in 1982.

there was inadequate tax planning. For example, the late Howard Hunt left an estate of about $460 million. The death taxes on his estate were 77% because he died in 1976 without a will.

An investment in antiques is valued at "fair market value" in an estate. The value is arrived at by appraisers usually appointed by the court. The administrator of an estate may hire a professional antique appraiser if the amount involved justifies the expenditure of his fee. The final appraisal figure will be based upon the amount which your estate or heirs could fairly expect to receive if they were to offer the antiques for sale on the open market. That is, fair market value is the price at which the antiques would exchange hands between a willing buyer and a willing seller. Thus, fair market value is the price at which the antiques could be sold at retail rather than dealers' prices. However, if the executor has to sell the antiques for less than fair market value, part of this difference may be deducted.

The contents of a home are considered in an estate. Since one of the outstanding advantages of being knowledgeable about and collecting antiques either as an investment or a hobby is the opportunity to furnish one's own home with pieces of highest quality, the homeowner-investor may lose sight of the fact that he may have a large percentage of his estate tax exemption in the "fair market value" of his home furnishings. An example of how rapidly home furniture can appreciate is in order. A young couple decided to furnish their living room, dining room, and part of one bedroom with modestly priced antiques. Over a period of three years they spent $1,000 to accomplish this end. When the furniture was professionally appraised, it was valued at over $4,000. In a large home with several decades to collect, trade, and upgrade, the "fair market value" could easily exceed $30,000, even if the original purchase price was only one or two thousand.

A loophole in the tax law is sufficiently important to mention briefly. When an estate is settled, the heirs receive the estate assets at a stepped-up basis. Thus, the appreciation in any estate assets escape the federal income tax. For example, assume that a decedent dies in 1982 owning a round oak table valued at

Increasing from a value of $3,500 in 1970 to $17,000 in 1980, this 1931 Model A Ford convertible cabriolet would have been an excellent investment. Antiques are not like savings account and other interest-bearing investments which are taxed at ordinary rates each year. If the owner dies owning such a car, the beneficiary will receive a stepped-up in basis and any appreciation would completely escape the federal income tax. (Photo courtesy of Old Cars Price Guide *magazine, Iola, Wisconsin)*

$800.00. The decedent had purchased the table for $5.00. The table would be included in the estate at $800.00 for federal estate tax purposes, and the heir would receive a stepped-up basis of $800.00 in the table. In other words, the $795.00 appreciation ($800 − 5.00) would escape the federal income tax. If the heir later sells the table for $850, he would recognize only a $50 gain ($850 − 800). Thus, one benefit of dying is that your heirs will receive a step-up in basis in any estate assets.

A danger facing many antique investors and traders is that upon their death no one in their family will have sufficient knowledge of which antiques are valuable and which are not. Often the other family members have no interest in the antiques. Thus, you must keep a complete inventory of all antiques at all times. Make certain your spouse or family knows where it is in case something should unexpectedly happen to you. There have been many valuable collections destroyed due to ignorance of their value. Everyone should have a will. In it a person, called an "executor," should be designated to settle your affairs upon your death. He or she should know about your antique investments. If you do not have a will, it would be wise to contact an attorney and have one drawn. At the same time, if you are near the $175,000 estate tax level (in 1981) referred to above, you should request further information on "estate planning" so that a possible savings can be made by avoiding the full impact of the estate tax.

There is a probate court in every legal jurisdiction which concerns itself with the administration of your estate at your death. You may write yourself a will before you die, or the state will write you a will if you die without a will (i.e., intestate). The probate court will inventory your assets and pay your liabilities. Anything left after expenses and estate tax will go to your heirs. Obviously probate is open to the public and is costly.

There are three major ways assets can flow outside the probate system directly to the heirs. First, property may be held jointly with rights of survivorship. Second, life insurance can be named payable to a beneficiary other than the estate. Third, assets may be held in a "living trust."

Joint ownership with rights of survivorship may not be advantageous. The bank may "lock" a safe deposit box on the death of one of the joint owners. Furthermore, both parties may die in a common accident.

Norman Dacey, the author of *How to Avoid Probate—Updated* ($15.95, Probate, Naugatuck, CT 06770), explains in detail this process of avoiding probate. He indicates how to avoid probate for most assets. For example, Chapter 11 deals with various declarations of trust designed to allow a safe deposit box to avoid the probate process.

GENERAL TIP If your furniture is antique or if you have fine family heirlooms, get a professional appraisal. The small fee will be well worthwhile since you will know the value of your possessions. You may also want to consider "fine arts" insurance protection for your fine heirlooms.

TAX TIP Keep accurate inventories of your antique investment. Make certain that someone else knows the location of your will and antique inventory.

Save Taxes by Making Lifetime Gifts

Under certain circumstances taxes can be saved by making lifetime gifts. This is especially true as the value of your assets increases and you grow older. If you plan to leave your antiques to your children upon your death, you may want to make gifts while you are still living. There may be certain tax advantages to a systematic giving program. If your estate is approaching the $175,000 level (in 1981) you may wish to consider reducing the value of your estate by making lifetime gifts. If you are in a high income tax bracket and you have children or others to whom you would like to make gifts (who are probably in lower income tax brackets than you), you may obtain both savings in income tax and estate tax by giving antiques and other assets to them. If they would receive the antiques eventually anyhow, and you have no real financial need now, you may wish to gain the tax benefits and at the same time see them enjoy your antiques during your lifetime.

Since making gifts is an obvious method of avoiding the estate tax at your death, the government imposes a tax on gift transfers in order to partially plug this escape route. However, you can still make gifts without incurring this tax. You are allowed to make tax free gifts of $10,000 ($3,000 before 1982) to *each* person during *each* year, plus an extra $175,000 ($47,000 unified credit in 1981) at any time during your life. Further, if both spouses consent on the gift tax return to split their gifts, all gifts to *third parties* are considered as having been made one-half by each spouse. You may find it advantageous to make gifts as time goes by.

A combination of the annual exclusion, the specific exemption, and the gift-splitting election allows a donor to transfer a great deal of property to family members and thereby escape the federal estate tax. For example, a husband and wife could transfer $2.4 million of tax-free gifts to their three sons and their wives over a ten-year period (if they die in 1987 and thereafter). The calculation of this tax-free amount is supplied below:

$20,000 annual exclusion x 6	$ 120,000	per year
Times	x 10	years
Tax-free gifts of	$1,200,000	
Husband's equivalent exemption	600,000	
Wife's equivalent exemption	600,000	
	$2,400,000	

This illustration should demonstrate the advantages of planned and systematic inter vivos giving.

You may wish to consider a transfer under the Gifts of Securities to Minors Act. In the typical situation the donor irrevocably transfers antiques or other assets to a minor by registering the property in the name of a custodian designated by the donor. To be sure the property will not be included in the donor's estate, the donor should *not* be the custodian. Make your wife or someone else the custodian.

The donor must be able to prove that gifts are in fact made. For example, one father wished to leave several of his ivory figurines to each of his minor children. He identified the figurines by clearly labeling each child's initials under various figurines contained in his collection. But all of the figurines continued to remain in his safe deposit box. Here the I.R.S. refused to agree that the gifts had in fact been completed.

Estate tax benefits are not the only advantage of a gift to a minor. In 1981, a minor can receive up to $3,300 of income tax-free. If a child is under 19 or a college student of any age and if the parents continue to provide more than one-half of his support, *both* he and his parents can claim him for a personal exemption. But the child can*not* qualify for a standard deduction (the $2,300 zero bracket amount) against this unearned income or from wages. A shift of income-producing property to a child can therefore result in a small income tax savings. Further, such gifts can insulate assets from the clutches of creditors. This income tax savings can be diluted where the donor has the obligation to support the donee. Regardless of the relationship of the donor or of the custodian to the donee, income from the gift property used to discharge the donor's support obligation is taxable to the donor.

A major expense of a family is the rising cost of sending a son or daughter to a college or university. This expenditure can be paid with antiques, possibly with a second collection. At the same time, you can save federal and state income taxes.

Here is how this strategy works. Suppose you have a son and/or daughter who is about to go off to college. There are many expenses. At the same time, you have an antique collection.

Give the antique collection to your child. Remember that you can give $10,000 *per year* ($20,000 if you are married) to *each* child without having to file a gift tax return. Technically, you can give more than $10,000 [$20,000] to a child per year without having to pay a gift tax, due to a so-called unified credit. There is no certification to prove a gift. But if a gift exceeds $10,000 ($20,000) to any donee during a taxable year, be sure *the parent* files a gift tax return and pays any gift tax. Surprisingly, the *donor* (and not the donee) has to pay any gift tax.

The child, after some time has passed (a month or two), asks you to sell the collection to an antique firm. You or your child sell the antiques at an auction or to a firm. The money is then used by the child to pay college expenses.

What about any gain on the sale of the antiques? Well, your son or daughter picks up your tax basis in the collection. For example, suppose the parent's tax basis is $500 and the collection is sold by the child for $4,000. The child is taxed on this $3,500 gain at capital gain rates (assuming the child is not a dealer). The child is probably in a much lower tax bracket than the parents, so there is a significant tax savings at the state and federal level.

This technique can be quite significant where there is a chance that the parent will be classified as a dealer in antiques. If a parent was an antique dealer and sold the antiques (without giving them to his child), the parent would be taxed as ordinary income on any gain.

Remember that you can give $10,000 ($20,000 if married) *each year* to a child without having to file a gift tax return. But *do not* give loss antiques away. Give only appreciated collectibles. If you give away loss assets, a special basis rule keeps both the parent or child from obtaining any deductible loss.

A technique upheld by the U. S. Court of Appeals for the Ninth Circuit should be of interest to antique dealers. Although this court case dealt with a physician, a dealer should be able to adopt this same technique of using a guardianship to split income among his children.

In the facts of the court case, a physician gave his children (ages 6 to 14) his business real estate, including his own medical building. The State Probate Court appointed the physician the guardian for the children, and he paid himself (as guardian for his children) the reasonable rental value of his medical office. These rent payments were used to pay for the children's health insurance, and education. As might be expected, the I.R.S. asserted that the real estate transfer lacked a business purpose and, therefore, the physician could not obtain a tax deduction for the rental payments.

The court disagreed with the I.R.S. It accepted the following non-tax motives as sufficient business purposes for the transfer: his desire to provide for the health and education of his children, avoidance of friction with partners in his medical practice, withdrawal of his assets from the threat of malpractice suits, and reduction of the ethical conflict arising from a physician being the landlord for a pharmacy.

In this same court case the I.R.S. also sought to tax the physician on the income he used for education and other expenses of his children. This is the typical ploy of the I.R.S. where funds of a trust are used to discharge the legal obligation of a parent to support his children. Again this court declined to go along, opining that the items involved were over and above the support state law required of the father.

An antique dealer could possibly split income from his antique operation by giving his children his business real estate, including his antique shop. Obviously the antique dealer must have non-tax reasons for such transfers and must document such reasons. The dealer could lease the antique shop back from his children. The children would be taxed on the rental income (at lower tax rates), and the dealer could deduct such rental payments as an ordinary and necessary business expense. Warning: For federal estate tax purposes, the fact that the father is the custodian of the property would cause the property to be included in his gross estate if the father dies *before* his children reach age 21. Thus, it may be wise to appoint someone else as the custodian, such as the mother.

Tax Tips

1. Gifts may save you federal estate taxes, state inheritance taxes, and federal and state income taxes.
2. Due to peculiar carryover basis rules, a donor should not give away antiques which have a loss value. He should sell these antiques, take the loss, and give the proceeds.
3. An elderly donor may find it is more advantageous *not* to give highly appreciated antiques since his beneficiaries receive a step-up in basis for any antiques transferred at death.
4. Since a donee can increase the basis of gift property by gift

taxes paid by the donor, the donee should retain adequate records to substantiate the donor's basis, the fair market value of the property at the date of the gift, and the amount of the gift tax paid. The donee should retain such information as long as he retains the gift property.

CHAPTER 10

Ownership Sets Taxes

One decision often facing a taxpayer is whether to hold antiques and other property in joint names or to have separate ownership. There are various types of joint ownership of property.

Tenancy by the entirety with rights of survivorship occurs between a husband and wife. This form of joint ownership cannot be destroyed by a transfer by only one of the spouses.

Joint tenancy with rights of survivorship occurs between nonspouses. Under this joint ownership, if one of the co-tenants dies, the entire ownership interest passes to the other co-tenant. The deceased party does not have anything to pass along or to leave by will to anyone. Neither co-tenant may destroy the joint ownership by transferring the interest, and neither can force a division or sale of the entire property.

Before 1977 under both a tenancy by the entirety and joint tenancy, each party was viewed as owning all of the property upon the death of the other co-tenant.

A tenancy in common (without rights of survivorship) is an undivided interest which can be transferred during life or at death. At death the applicable portion of the undivided interest is included in the gross estate. Community property occurs in seven states where each spouse is viewed as having a one-half vested property right. At death one-half of the community property is included in the gross estate and taxed by the federal estate tax.

Real estate is generally held in joint ownership rather than separately. But non-real estate such as rare coins, stamps, antiques, jewelry, etc., can be held jointly.

A special election is available under the tax law before 1982 with respect to real property. A donor (spouse) may elect to treat one-half of a transfer of real property to a tenancy by the entirety as a gift, reportable by the donor on a gift tax return. Since one-half of a joint tenancy created after 1976 is automatically excluded from the gross estate, this special election is of questionable value since there is the immediate loss of any gift taxes payable. Possibly if the individual believes the real estate will appreciate significantly or the initial gift tax is small, this special election may be worthwhile.

Under prior law (before 1982) the gross estate included 100 percent of the value of all property owned in joint tenancy with the rights of survivorship. However, if any part of the property or its acquisition cost is traceable to the survivor, that portion of the value of the property may be excluded from the gross estate. For example, any property acquired jointly by the decedent and another joint owner through a gift is included in the decedent's gross estate only to the extent of the decedent's fractional share of such property. These rules apply to all classes of property, whether real or personal, but do not apply to property held as tenants in common.

The rules for property held jointly by spouses with survivorship rights have been simplified for tax years after 1981. Each spouse is to be treated as one-half owner of joint tenancy assets regardless of which spouse furnished the funds to acquire the property or regardless of how the joint tenancy was created. Thus, the first spouse to die will include one-half of the joint tenancy in gross estate, and only one-half of any separate property will receive a step-up in basis.

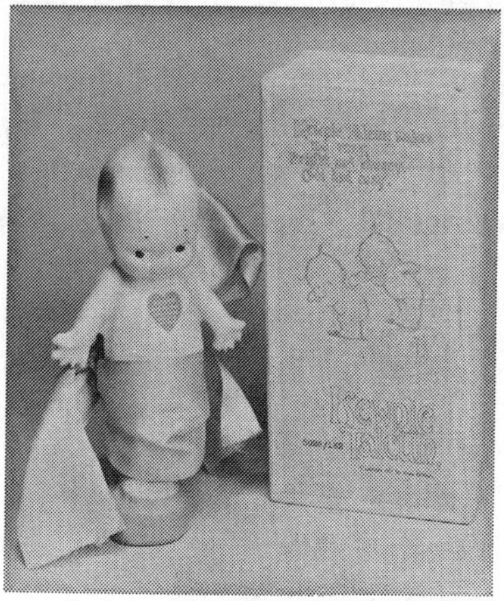

Even housewares have become collectible and therefore valuable. This little Kewpie Doll Talcum Powder doll and box originally sold for about 75¢ in 1917; it's worth $100 to $150 today. Such rises in value have not escaped the attention of Uncle Sam's agents. (Photo courtesy of Mapes Auctioneers/ Appraisers, Vestal, New York)

Joint ownership of property by married couples may no longer be appropriate because of the unlimited marital deduction. However, with the current high divorce rate, who is to own the property?

An international accounting firm, Deloitte, Haskins & Sells, indicates that there are several advantages of joint ownership as compared with separate ownership:

Sense of family security in that the property is not owned by any one individual but by the family (husband and wife) as a whole.

Convenience and safety since either party may enjoy and use the property without the permission of the other.

In the case of property held in joint tenancy or tenancy by the entirety, the property passes to the surviving tenant on death without going through the deceased's probate estate, which can yield a savings in executor's fees and other estate administration costs. In addition, in many states, certain jointly-owned property would not be available to creditors of the deceased.

This same accounting firm indicates that there are two major disadvantages of co-ownership:

Loss of Control—Where more than one person owns property, the control and use of the property is shared by the joint owners and no one individual generally has the legal right to restrict the other owners in their use and enjoyment of the property.

Dispositions at Death—In cases where a right of survivorship exists, the deceased cannot dispose of his property by his will since the co-owner automatically takes full ownership of the property. Even if no right of survivorship exists, the deceased can only convey his interest in the property through his will rather than the entire property.

CHAPTER 11

Installment Tax Method

An investor, collector, or dealer may defer any gain on the sale of antiques by using the installment tax method. Rules for the installment method were simplified and liberalized in 1980. Suppose you decide to sell your antique collection and/or one or more antiques. If you are not a dealer in antiques, the installment tax method may effect a tax savings. (A dealer falls within another installment tax method.) If the buyer pays you with at least one payment in a tax year after the year of sale, you automatically qualify for installment treatment. Remember, an installment contract must contain a minimum nine percent annual interest in order to avoid having the I.R.S. impute an interest income amount in a transaction.

To understand the advantage of this election it is important to know how to compute the taxable income in one year from the formula below:

$$\frac{\text{Total Profit (selling price less costs \& basis)}}{\text{Installment Contract Price}} \times \text{Payments during the year}$$

For example, suppose on December 2, 1980, you sold an American chippendale card and game table for $1,500, which had cost you $250 in 1970. If you had received a down payment of $180 in December, $480 in 1981, and the remainder in the next year, you would recognize the following taxable gains in the respective years:

In 1980 $$\frac{1500-250}{1500} \times \$180 = \$150$$

In 1981 $$\frac{1500-250}{1500} \times \$480 = \$150$$

In 1982 $$\frac{1500-250}{1500} \times \$840 = \$700$$

As this example illustrates, any gain from the sale of the chippendale table is spread over a three-year period. Spreading gains over a number of years will normally result in a net tax savings. Where a sale results in a loss, the installment method is not used.

A collector or investor may wish to elect out of the installment method when the tax liability is less under income averaging. That is, you may wish to receive all payments in one year and income average your capital gain. You will have to make the tax calculations both ways.

An antique dealer may also elect to report gross profit earned on installment sales for tax purposes under another type of installment method. Again under this installment method any gross profit realized by a dealer on an installment sale is taxed at the point the cash is collected from his customer.

The tax law defines an "installment sale" as a sale of personal property under terms that contemplate that the sale will be paid for in two or more installments and the purchase is, in fact, paid for in two or more installments. If an antique dealer sells on credit without any arrangement for installment payments, he must normally use the accrual method and cannot use the installment method. However, traditional installment plans (e.g., separate

Country furniture, with accessories such as the hooked rug, which itself might be worth anywhere from $25 to $250. The pine jelly cupboard might today bring $250, if in nice condition. Original finish is important. (Photo courtesy of Mapes Auctioneers/Appraisers, Vestal, New York)

contracts providing for payments over a specific time period) normally qualify for this special installment break.

Where a dealer is presently using the accrual method for tax purposes and has a significant amount of installment sales, a change to the installment tax method will result in a semi-permanent increase in working capital. The deferred profit causes a corresponding postponement of a dealer's income tax—an interest-free loan from the government.

One of the unfavorable aspects of the law changes in 1980 dealing with the installment method involves sales to related parties. The purpose of these complicated new rules was to stop certain techniques involving sales to related parties, followed by a gift or forgiveness of the indebtedness. Although these rules are quite harmful to stocks and securities, antiques and other collectibles (along with land) can still be used effectively.

Here is how an antique collector or dealer could transfer his antiques to his heirs and avoid any estate or gift taxes. Suppose a parent sells his antique collection to his two children for $600,000 on July 3, 1980. The collection has a basis of $50,000 and was held as an investment. Parent will receive 9% interest-bearing notes payable $10,000 per year ($20,000 if parent is married). As each payment becomes due, parent forgives the note.

There are some valuable advantages of these installment sales/gifts. First, this technique spreads the gifts over a number of years in order to take advantage of the $10,000 exclusion ($20,000 if married) to avoid any gift tax. Second, the children are vested immediately with absolute ownership. Thus, any subsequent appreciation in the collection is not included in the parents estate (i.e., escapes the federal estate tax). Third, the children receive a step-up in basis equal to the selling price. Fourth, any gain on the antiques is spread over the duration of the pay-off by the children (i.e., deferral of the tax liability).

An alternative strategy is to sell the collection to the children with a balloon payment many years later (i.e., 25 years). Due to inflation, the children will pay off the liability with very cheap dollars. This strategy allows assets to be transferred from one generation to the next generation with little estate tax payable.

Congress attempted to eliminate these sales among related parties. In general, a related party includes spouses, children, grandchildren, and parents. Under the new law effective after May 14, 1980, any gain to be reported under the installment method is accelerated where a related party resells property within two years of the initial installment sale. Here is the interesting point: this resale rule applies without any time limitation for sale of stocks and securities. Thus, antiques, other collectibles, and land appear to be excellent assets to be used with this estate transfer scheme. This law may cause even more monies to be withdrawn from the stock markets and invested in investment collectibles and land.

CHAPTER 12

Trade Those Antiques

High income tax rates have made it almost a daily occurrence for most real estate brokers to advise their customers to trade their real estate holdings for properties which they wish to acquire, rather than to sell what they have and then buy for cash. Trading one investment for another of like-kind property involves no gain for income tax purposes.

Trading rather than selling antiques can result in a definite tax advantage. Trading can easily be accomplished by joining an exchange service or exchanging antiques with fellow collectors in antique clubs. However, eventually the I.R.S. will collect the taxes (unless the investor dies before he sells the antiques, in which case the heirs obtain a stepped-up basis). When he finally decides to sell rather than trade, any gain for income tax purposes depends upon what he paid for the first item traded. The basis in each antique is transferred to the items for which it is traded.

Trading allows an individual to postpone the tax burden to a later date. This delay may bring important advantages. A trade can forestall the expense of the tax until a time when the individual is in a better position to bear it, or until he is in a lower overall tax bracket. Remember, any tax liability which he is able to postpone increases his cash flow, and he can earn interest or other investment incomes on this postponed tax (e.g., invest in more antiques, stamps, stock, etc.). Think of a postponement of your tax liability as an interest-free loan from the federal government.

Antiques that have decreased in value below an investor's tax basis should *not* be traded. If he trades loss antiques, any potential deductible loss is postponed for tax purposes, just as any gain would be postponed. The best tax strategy for loss antiques is to sell the antique so that losses are immediately deductible. The investor may use the proceeds from the sale of his loss antique to purchase the antique which he wanted with the trade.

Where you receive "boot" (other property or money) in such an exchange, you must recognize any gain the extent of such "boot." The holding period for the new antique received in exchange includes the holding period of the old antique.

You must actually exchange one antique for another antique. You may not defer the gain by merely selling one antique and reinvesting the proceeds into another antique.

For example, you trade a Louis XV sofa for which you paid \$300 a number of years ago for an American Queen Anne tilt table for about \$900. You also receive cash of \$100 from the dealer. There is a gain of about \$700 on the transaction (\$1,000 – \$300), but only \$100 is taxable to you. Technically, a taxable gain in a trade is recognized (taxed) at the *lower* of (1) the actual gain, or (2) the fair market value of the boot received. Of course, your basis in the new antique is calculated as follows: Old basis *minus* boot received *plus* any gain recognized. Thus, the tilt table will have a \$300 basis (\$300 – \$100 + \$100).

An antique dealer may trade business assets (i.e., automobile) for a like-kind asset and postpone any potential taxable gain. However, a like-kind exchange is not available for inventory assets. For example, an antique dealer can*not* trade inventory antiques for other antiques in order to avoid any taxable gain.

CHAPTER 13

Investments During Economic Crises

One measure of the value of a particular investment is how it might perform during difficult economic times. Of course, during a recession the investment rules change. One book on this subject, *How to Survive and Prosper in the Next American Depression, War or Revolution* (Financial Management Associates, Inc., 3824 East Indian School Road, Phoenix, AZ 85018), provides some insight into the problems during a recession.

This FMA book provides a chart of the behavior of a composite index of valuables during a depression. The relationship of valuables may be divided into three categories. Each category behaves differently. The first category is very high priced items recognized as particularly desirable. The FMA book placed American Colonial and Federalist antique furniture, first-quality large diamonds, and paintings by the old masters in this first category.

During a depression these high value items drop, but the drop is relatively less sharp and the recovery comes faster and higher. Why? Owners are reluctant to sell them, and they are quickly bought by people who still have money.

A second category consists of items that are commonly recognized as valuable but are not "cream of the crop." They are

Currier and Ives prints originally sold for pennies. Fire-fighting and sailing scenes are particularly desired today, with the large folio-size frequently bringing several hundreds of dollars. Such increases in value do not escape the attention of the tax man. (Photo courtesy of Mapes Auctioneers/Appraisers, Vestal, New York)

rare but not unique. This category includes things such as large diamonds not of first quality, Colonial country furniture, good paintings not by old masters, and some types of oriental art. These medium valued items have a much sharper drop to a much deeper low, followed by a gradual, steady recovery.

Items in the second category are sold by their owners more quickly when trouble develops because the owners know they can replace them when they have money again. This category has a thick market with much less support for the prices. Buyers do not see these items as bargains worth acquiring until the prices have dropped to relatively low levels. On the other hand, there is

Rare coins and stamps can be kept safely in a safe deposit box as they appreciate yearly. The 1981 "Red Book" indicates that an 1892 half-dollar in MS-60 condition would retail at $800. The $5 black Alexander Hamilton stamp was issued on March 19, 1956, and the 1981 Scott's catalogue (Scott #1053) lists a price of $150 for an unused issue. (Stamp picture courtesy of Harris Stamp Co., Boston, Massachusetts. Coin picture courtesy of Bowers & Ruddy Galleries, Los Angeles, California)

a fair amount of interest in them and so once the price drops low enough they are purchased as fast as they come on the market.

The third category of items are fashionable, collectible, and have a thin market. They are either not high quality specimens or are seen as minor. This category includes most antique jewelry, products of modern artists, art made for export, and similar items.

The low value items never really develop a market. Their prices collapse and never really recover. They have the fastest of all price drops and almost no recovery.

The low value items are either things that are of interest only to specialist collectors or they are inferior samples of the genre. Their owners see them as eminently disposable in a crisis and feel no desire to replace them with similar items when the crisis has passed. If they are still interested in that kind of thing, they prefer to replace them with medium value items which have dropped enough in price to be available.

One final "food for thought." The 1929 crash was coupled with deflation. Any future depression may be involved with inflation.

CHAPTER 14

Tax Benefits of Gift Giving

Contributions to certain organizations which fall under the qualification outlined in the Internal Revenue Code Section 501(c) (which include charities, educational, and scientific institutions) are deductible in 1981 from a taxpayer's adjusted gross income, which means, of course, that taxpayers should be sure to make charitable contributions in years in which they have enough itemized deductions to exceed their standard deduction. In general, a charitable contribution is worth the marginal tax bracket of an individual. For example, if you are in the 40% marginal tax bracket, a $1,000 contribution to a Section 501(c) organization is worth $400 on your federal income tax return.

Beginning in 1982, a portion of a charitable contribution shall be a deduction for adjusted gross income. In other words, individuals who do not itemize deductions may deduct the following percentage of their charitable contributions, subject to the respective overall limitation:

Year	Percentage Contribution Limitation	Overall Limitation
1982	25%	$100
1983	25	100
1984	25	300
1985	50	none
1996	100	none

General Provisions

There are certain limitations imposed upon charitable contributions made by an individual. These limitations are quite complex, and in order to appreciate them, you must first understand that there are two types of Section 501(c) organizations: the public organization and the private organization. Gifts to public organizations qualify for the 50 percent ceiling; to such public organizations an individual can deduct up to 50 percent of his "contribution base," and contributions in excess of this ceiling can be carried over for the next five tax years. A person's "contribution base" is his adjusted gross income disregarding any net operating loss carryback. Section 501(c) organizations qualifying for the 50 percent ceiling include most churches and universities, American Red Cross, United Fund, Boy Scouts, Salvation Army, and many other well-known charities and institutions. Ask the potential organization if contributions to them qualify for a deduction when you are in doubt. Merely because an organization is tax exempt does not automatically mean it is qualified to fall under Section 501(c).

All other qualified organizations which are not in the 50 percent bracket are 20 percent organizations. These 20 percent organizations are private foundations or organizations, but not private operating foundations. Gifts to 20 percent organizations are deductible up to the lesser of 20 percent of the taxpayer's contribution base, or 50 percent of his contribution base minus contributions to 50 percent organizations (including carryovers of such contributions and with no reduction for the 30 percent ceiling on appreciated property). For example, if a person contributes 38 percent of his contribution base to a 50 percent organization (for example, a church), his contributions to 20 percent organizations are deductible only up to 12 percent of his contribution base. Furthermore, he is not allowed to carry over any excess gifts to 20 percent organizations.

Contribution of Appreciated Property

There are three sets of tax rules for all contributions of appreciated property (that is, all property which would give rise to any gain if sold, such as precious gems, stocks, bonds, stamp collections, and antiques):

1. ordinary income-type property,
2. tangible personal capital gain property, and contributions of capital gain property to certain private foundations, and
3. appreciated capital gain property.

Property whose appreciation would not be all long-term capital gain to the contributor, if he sold it at its fair market value on the date it was contributed, falls into this first category of ordinary income-type property. For charitable contribution of any property which gives rise to any ordinary income appreciation on disposition, the property's fair market value on the date of contribution is reduced by the amount of ordinary income appreciation in order to determine the deductible amount. Inventory, letters, and memoranda given by a person who prepared them, and works of art donated by the artist who created them, fall within this category. For example, a person purchases stock in 1981 for $2,500 and contributes it to a church four months later when it is worth $4,000. Since the $1,500 of appreciation is short-term gain, his charitable deduction is only $2,500 ($4,000 – $1,500). If, however, the stock was held at least 12 months and one day and then contributed to the church, this transaction would fall within the third category, and there would be no reduction in the appreciation.

Obviously, an individual should avoid gifts of short-term and ordinary income property to Section 501(c) organizations whenever possible. An individual should leave this type of property to an organization in his will in order to obtain a full estate tax deduction. Or else, he may wish to leave the property to his children, who will get a step-up in their tax basis, and they can then give the property to a qualified organization and obtain a larger income deduction.

Into the second category fall two types of transactions. First, if the asset contributed is tangible personal property, its utilization by the recipient organization must be directly related to the exempt function of the organization in order to qualify for the full deduction. If not directly related to the exempt function of the organization, then the deduction is limited to cost plus 60 percent of the appreciation for non-corporate donors (the percentage becomes 39.13 percent for corporate donors). For example, a stamp collection has a cost basis of $2,500 and a fair market value of $4,000. The collection was held three years and then given to a church which sells it in order to use the proceeds. Since the collection is not directly related to the exempt function of the church, the deduction would be limited to a cost of $2,500 plus 60 percent of the appreciation, $900—a total deduction of $3,400. However, if the collection was donated to a university *to be used for educational purposes,* the donor would be entitled to a larger $4,000 deduction.

Thus, whether a contribution is for an "unrelated use" or "directly related use" to a Section 501(c) organization is very important to the taxpayer. The term "unrelated use" means a use which is unrelated to the purpose or function constituting the basis for the organization's tax exemption. For instance, if a precious gem collection contributed to an educational institution is used by that organization for educational purposes by being placed in its li-

This 1930 four-cylinder Model A Ford sedan, restored to its original conditions and colors (Kiwanee green and Elkpoint green), was voted "Best of Show" at the Santa Clara Valley Chapter of the Model A Ford Annual Restoration Meeting in 1977. From 1970 to 1980, such an antique car appreciated at an annual rate of 12%. This appreciation could be transferred to a child for educational purposes, and the gain would be taxed in a lower tax bracket. (Photo courtesy of Old Cars Price Guide *magazine, Iola, Wisconsin; car owned at the time by Mr. and Mrs. Ed Enos of San Jose, California)*

brary for display and study by the students, the use is not an unrelated use. But if the collection is sold and the proceeds used by the organization for education purposes, the use of the property is an "unrelated use." If, however, a collection is contributed to a charitable organization or governmental unit, and the donee sells or otherwise disposes of only an insubstantial portion of the collection, the use could still be considered "related." Obviously, potential donors of appreciated tangible personal property must match the item of property to be given with the appropriate recipient organization.

A second type of transaction will cause a 40 percent reduction in the appreciation of appreciated property. If capital gain property is given to a private foundation (not a private operating foundation or community foundation) which does not make qualifying distributions equal to the amount of such contributions within two and one-half months after the close of the year, then the deduction is limited to the property's fair market value minus 40 percent of the appreciation.

Directly Related to Exempt Function

A third category involves the contribution to a Section 501(c) organization of appreciated capital gain property which is directly related to the exempt function of the organization. Capital gain property is a capital asset which, if sold at the time contributed, would give rise only to long-term capital gain. Certain property used in a trade or business, precious and semi-precious stones, coins, stamps, antiques, art work, etc., qualify as capital gain property. When a taxpayer contributes such property to a qualified organization, his deduction ceiling is reduced to 30 percent for the property rather than the normal 50 percent, unless the taxpayer makes a special election to reduce the amount of his contribution. In other words, the total amount of contribution of capital gain property considered for deduction purposes for any tax year cannot exceed 30 percent of the taxpayer's contribution base (generally adjusted gross income). When an individual makes a special election his deduction ceiling remains at 50 percent along with a 50 percent carryover, but the taxpayer may deduct only the capital gain property's basis plus 50 percent of any appreciation.

For example, assume that Chuck Charitable, who has an $11,000 adjusted gross income, makes a charitable contribution of part of his antique collection to a museum for display purposes during 1981. The portion of the collection contributed has a tax basis of $2,000 but is valued at $10,000. During 1981 Chuck may deduct

$3,300 (30% of $11,000), which leaves him a contribution carryover of $6,700 (but subject to the 30% carryover rule). On the other hand, if Chuck so desires, he may elect to have his contribution be $6,000 ($2,000 basis plus 50 percent of $8,000 appreciation). Here he could deduct $5,500 during 1981 (50% × $11,000) with a contribution carryover of $500 (subject to the 50 percent carryover rule). A taxpayer probably would not elect the 50 percent rule where he makes a contribution of highly appreciated capital gain property, and of course, a taxpayer who owns property worth substantially less than its cost basis should sell it and then contribute the proceeds to the organization.

If a person contributes any property to a Section 501(c) organization and pays an appraisal fee to someone in order to determine the fair market value of his property, the appraisal expenses are deductible from his adjusted gross income, provided he itemizes his deductions and does not use the zero bracket amount.

Determining Value of the Collection

One major problem in figuring contribution deductions is the determination of the fair market value of a donated item or collection. The law indicates that the value is the amount for which the material could be sold between a reasonable buyer and a reasonable seller (within a reasonable period of time). Consider a contribution of precious stones to a charitable organization: Do you use the value as shown in the *Blue Book* or *PreciouStone Newsletter,* from a laboratory such as United States Gemological Laboratory, an independent appraisal, or in the case of a diamond, one of the price matrices listed in the Monday's commodities section of *The Wall Street Journal,* or some other authoritative source? In determining the economic values of precious gems, it is important to determine their value in the highest market. Thus, the fair market value of a collection depends to a great extent on where and how it is sold. For instance, if we assume that a collector has a small diamond collection that he wishes to contribute to an organization, the hypothetical "market value" of the collection might be as follows:

Sold to a neighborhood jeweler	$100,000
Listed in *PreciouStone Newsletter*	125,000
Sold at public auction as one lot	150,000
Listed in *Blue Book*	175,000
Subdivided into 5 lots and sold through different auctions	200,000

The hypothetical "market price" should no doubt be the highest of these figures. This same type of reasoning applies to most tangible assets.

Proof and Records

What proof of use should a taxpayer maintain? First, government regulations state that he may establish that the contributed property is not in fact put to an unrelated use by the Section 501(c) organization. Or second, he may establish that the property will not be put to an unrelated use by the organization. For example, in the case of a gift of a gem collection to a museum, if the donated stones are of a general type normally retained by such museum, it is reasonable for the taxpayer to anticipate (unless he has actual knowledge to the contrary) that the gems will not be put to an unrelated use by the museum, whether or not the stones are later sold or exchanged by the organization.

If a taxpayer makes a charitable contribution of appreciated property and claims a deduction in excess of $200, he must attach to his tax return the following information:

1. Name and address of the organization to which the contribution was made.

2. The date of the actual contribution.
3. A detailed description of the property along with the condition of the property.
4. The manner of acquisition (for example, purchase, gift, inheritance, etc.).
5. The fair market value of the property along with the method utilized in determining the fair market value and if there was an appraisal, a copy of the signed report of the appraiser.
6. The cost or adjusted basis of the property.
7. Where the deduction is reduced by any of the appreciation, the reduced amount.
8. Any agreement or understanding between the taxpayer and the organization and
9. The total amount claimed as a deduction for the next year.

Any deduction for a charitable contribution must be substantiated, when required by the district director of the Internal Revenue Service, by a statement from the organization to which the contribution was made indicating whether the organization is a domestic organization, the name and address of the contributor, the amount of the contribution, the date of actual receipt of the contribution, and such other information as the district director may deem necessary. When the property has a fair market value in excess of $200 at the time of receipt, the statement must also indicate for each item its location, if it is retained by the organization, the amount received by the organization of any sale of the property, and the date of sale, or, in case of any other disposition of the property by the organization, whether or not it is used for a purpose or function constituting the basis for the organization's exemption from income tax under Internal Revenue Code Section 501(c), or in the case of a government unit, whether or not it is used exclusively for public purposes.

An individual may not be willing to make a large charitable contribution to an organization during his lifetime; instead, the individual may wish to place the contribution in his will, to be executed upon his death. If such a testamentary contribution is made, the decedent will obtain a deduction on his federal estate tax return. However, since a gift to a qualified organization made during one's lifetime is deductible from one's income tax, a testamentary contribution is less beneficial because the income tax deduction is lost.

An estate tax charitable deduction is unlimited; an individual can give his entire estate to a Section 501(c) organization. (Under state law a surviving spouse and/or children may be entitled to a share of your estate. Obtain competent advice if you plan to disinherit your heirs.) A testamentary contribution is not subject to the 20%, 30%, or 50% restrictions which are applicable to the income tax deduction; in general the estate tax deduction is allowable to the extent of the fair market value of the donated property, and the deduction is not reduced by the amount (or part) of the gain that would have resulted from a sale of the asset.

If a person leaves cash or other assets outright in his will to some qualified organization, his estate will receive the expected deduction. If the contribution is other than cash, the amount of the deduction is based upon the fair market value. The deduction cannot exceed the actual value of the assets included in the decedent's gross estate.

If you are thinking of making a charitable contribution through your will, be sure to identify the organization accurately by its exact corporate name. You can then specify that your gift be used for a specific purpose, or make an outright gift to the organization without indicating a specific purpose.

Charitable Remainder Interest

The law has restricted the right to make gifts to Section 501(c) organizations and at the same time retain control or enjoyment of the property. At present a remainder interest is deductible only if it takes three forms: an annuity trust, a unitrust, or a pool income fund. Essentially you arrange for the organization to pay income to you and/or to your wife on the amount of your contribution as long as you live, with the property belonging to the charity on your death. While it is beyond the scope of this book to provide all of the rules about these three charitable remainder trusts, any charitable organization should be willing to provide you with the necessary forms and explanations. A short explanation of the three varieties, however, should give you an indication of the advantages of each.

Charitable remainder annuity trust is a trust that is to pay its income beneficiary (or beneficiaries) a specific sum which is not less than 5 percent of the initial fair market value of all property placed in the trust. At the death of the income beneficiary, or at the end of a term of years (not greater than 20 years), the remainder interest must be paid to a qualified organization.

Charitable remainder unitrust is a trust that is to pay the income beneficiary (or beneficiaries) a fixed percentage which is not less than 5 percent of the net fair market value of its assets (as valued annually). There are two exceptions. The trust instrument may provide (1) that the trustee is to pay the income beneficiary for any year an amount of trust income, where this amount is less than the portion required to be distributed by the particular unitrust, and (2) that the trustee is to pay the beneficiary an amount of trust income in excess of that required to be distributed to the extent he paid less than that portion in prior years because of the requirement to pay only the amount of the trust income.

Pooled income fund is similar to a charitable remainder trust except that the donor's irrevocable gifts are comingled with similar contributions in a fund maintained by the organization to which the remainder interest is contributed. This fund must meet six strict rules.

There are two exceptions for a future interest contribution. First, an individual can retain a life estate in a personal residence or a farm and still give the remainder to a qualified organization upon his death. Here the individual can obtain a significant charitable deduction on his income tax return. Second, an individual may make a bequest of a remainder interest that represents an undivided portion of his entire interest in the property. This latter exception applies in a situation where the decedent is the remainderman of a trust created by someone else (after a private life estate) and he gives a portion of the remainder to a Section 501(c) organization. An income tax deduction would be allowable.

Conclusion

Whenever an individual considers a charitable contribution, whether it be made during his lifetime or following his death, a basic understanding of the tax rules in this area is essential to attain maximum tax benefits. Wading through tax rulings can be a laborious and confusing task. It is hoped this chapter has outlined the principal categories involved in contributions which will enable the philanthropist, with the aid of his lawyer and accountant, to enjoy not only the humanitarian aspect of his giving but also some relief from taxation.

CHAPTER 15

Old Building Tax Shelter

Tax laws serve at least three functions—raise revenues, redistribute income, and promote (or discourage) certain social or economic activities. The Revenue Act of 1978 provided an example of an attempt to promote the restoration of existing structures and discourage the destruction of historically significant structures. This technique was liberalized by the Economic Recovery Tax Act of 1981 so that historic restoration is one of the best tax shelters available.

Under the new law a 3-tier investment credit is available for structures at least 30 years old. For expenditures incurred after December 31, 1981 a 15% tax credit is available for costs of rehabilitating commercial buildings that are 30 to 40 years old, a 20% credit for buildings that are at least 40 years old, and a 25% credit for rehabilitating certified residential or commercial historic structures.

As incentive for urban rehabilitation and renewal, the credit is available if the required rehabilitation is substantial. At least 75% of the existing external walls must be retained. A lessee is eligible for the tax credit if the remaining lease term is at least 15 years. The tax credit is not available for the purchase price, and any portion attributable to enlargement does not qualify.

Christmas collectibles, paper maché. Originally sold for a few cents, today they sometimes bring well over $100. (Photo courtesy of Mapes Auctioneers/ Appraisers, Vestal, New York)

This new rehabilitation credit applies in place of the regular investment tax credit and the energy tax credit. If a taxpayer uses the rehabilitation credit, the straight-line depreciation is required. Further, except for a certified historic building, the depreciable basis of the structure must be reduced by the amount of any rehabilitation tax credit taken.

Here is how you can take advantage of this latest tax shelter. Find an old but sound structure that needs extensive internal work and trade for it as a tax-free exchange. Then completely renovate it, taking advantage of the appropriate rehabilitation credit. Open an antique shop in the renovated building; a taxpayer or a member of the taxpayer's family may not use the property for residential purposes.

For example, assume that you incur $100,000 of eligible rehabilitation expenditures on a 40-year-old building. The available rehabilitation tax credit would be $20,000, but the depreciable basis would be $80,000, subject to straight-line depreciation. If this was a certified historic building, the basis would not have to be reduced. The Secretary of the Interior may classify an individual structure as a certified historic structure, but a building in a historic district *is* a certified historic structure.

If there is an early disposition of a rehabilitated building, there is a recapture penalty. Any recapture amount will increase the structure's basis for depreciation purposes.

Now you can restore and rehabilitate the historic character of a building and obtain a nice credit which lowers the after-tax cost of rehabilitating the structure.

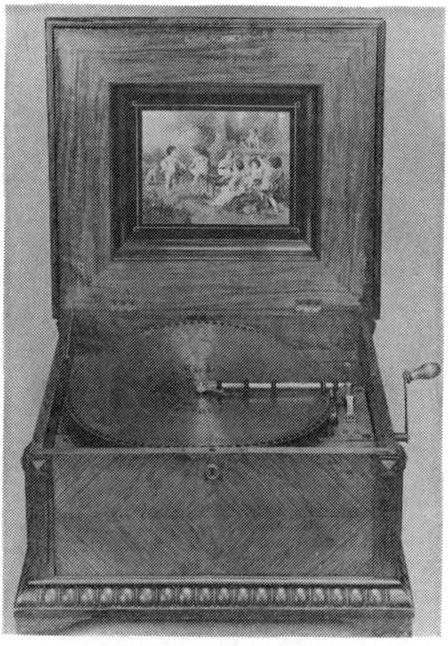

Few items have appreciated as well as automatic music machines, such as this Polyphon disk musical box which today is worth an easy $1,800 to $2,200. One expert has estimated that these instruments appreciated an average of around 17% per year between 1965 and 1981. (Photo courtesy of Mapes Auctioneers/Appraisers, Vestal, New York)

CHAPTER 16

Private Annuity

If you are about to retire and your retirement income will be small, a private annuity may be an effective tool for you to consider. You may be able to sell your antiques to a family member in return for fixed payments for your life. You allow someone else to enjoy your collection, and you have food on your table.

In such a transaction an annuitant (an owner of property) sells his property for an unsecured promise by the transferee to pay a fixed sum periodically for the life of the annuitant. According to the I.R.S., each fixed payment to the annuitant is composed of three elements: (1) a tax-free return of the annuitant's investment, (2) a recognized gain from the sale of the property (generally capital gain), and (3) interest income as a result of the delay in payment of the sale price.

If the fair market value of the assets transferred exceeds the present value of the annuity payment, there is a taxable gift to the transferee. Assuming the assets are transferred without retaining an interest (i.e., merely for an unsecured promise), the transferred assets are *not* included in the annuitant's gross estate.

Here is how a collector could use this technique. Mr. Sam Rarity is the owner of a significant pattern glass collection. He accumulated the collection over 30 years, paying a total cost of $40,000. The collection is now worth $600,000. In order to assure satisfactory income in his retirement years, Mr. Rarity sells his collection for an annuity of $60,000 (unsecured promise by his son). If Mr. Rarity is 56 years old, the present value of the annuity is approximately $600,000 (equal to the value of his collection).

Mr. Rarity's exclusion factor (element one above) is determined by using the typical annuity formula:

$$\frac{\textit{Investment in contract}}{\text{Annual Return x Multiple*}}$$

$$= \frac{40,000}{60,000} \text{ x } 21 = .031746$$

*This term "multiple" refers to the estimated remaining life of Mr. Rarity. The figure is found in tables provided by the I.R.S.

Thus, only $1,905 ($60,000 × .031746) of each $60,000 payment would be tax-free (i.e., excluded from Mr. Rarity's taxable income). His capital gain of $560,000 ($600,000 − $40,000) is divided by his life expectancy of 21 years in order to determine the capital gain portion of each $60,000 payment—or $26,667. The remainder, or $31,428 would be taxed as interest income (i.e., ordinary income).

To summarize, his $60,000 yearly receipts would be broken into these three elements:

Return of original investment (tax-free)	$ 1,905
Capital gain	26,667
Interest income	31,428
Total annual receipt	$60,000

There are some disadvantages of private annuities. First, if the annuitant (i.e., Mr. Rarity) does not live to his life expectancy, he

Country drop-front desk, perhaps from a small post office. Value range: chair, $125, desk $300. (Photo courtesy of Mapes Auctioneers/Appraisers, Vestal, New York)

has not received his investment back, yet he is paying taxes. Second, if he lives past his life expectancy, he continues to pay ordinary income tax on $31,428 per year. Third, the I.R.S. and the Tax Court indicates that the transferee is *not* allowed an interest expense deduction. Fourth, the annuitant must have only an *unsecured* promise to receive the annuity or else the annuity would be included in his gross estate. Of course, it is possible for Mr. Rarity (the annuitant) to purchase life insurance on the life of the transferee.

CHAPTER 17

Disposing of a Collection

You have several tax alternatives when disposing of an antique collection. Let us mention several of them and then discuss two of them.

1. You could sell it gradually, risking being classified as a dealer (with ordinary income).
2. You could sell it at one time and use the installment method to defer the overall capital gain tax.
3. You could sell it all in one year and use income averaging.
4. You could sell it to a relative in return for a private annuity (Chapter 16).
5. You could transfer the collection to a non-profit organization using a charitable remainder annuity trust.
6. You could receive an annuity issued by a charitable organization for your antique collection (a gift annuity).

Let us discuss this charitable remainder annuity trust. A charitable remainder annuity trust is a trust that is to pay its income beneficiary (you and your wife) a specific sum which is not less than 5% of the initial fair market value of all property (the antique

Toys don't have to be old to have risen greatly in value. Certain models of robots such as this one may bring hundreds of dollars at toy auctions. Without proper tax planning, anyone can easily become liable for taxes much higher than would have to be paid if suggestions throughout this book are heeded. (Photo courtesy of Mapes Auctioneers/ Appraisers, Vestal, New York)

collection) placed in the trust. At the death of the income beneficiary (you and your wife), or at the end of a term of years (not greater than 20 years), the remainder interest must be paid to the qualified organization (i.e. college).

For example, you may transfer your Currier & Ives prints to a charitable remainder annuity trust, reserve an annuity for you and your wife's lifetimes, and deduct the value of the remainder interest that eventually passes to your favorite college. The primary advantage of a contribution of a remainder interest is that you realize an immediate tax benefit from the charitable deduction but you and your wife will continue to enjoy income in the form of an annuity from the contributed print collection. The amount of the deduction that arises from the transfer of the print collection to the annuity trust is the excess of the fair market value of the collection placed in the trust over the present value of the annuity reserved by you and your wife. I.R.S. tables indicate how to determine the fair market value of the annuity.

Another alternative is the gift annuity. An annuity could be issued by a charitable organization for your antique collection. A gift annuity consists of the amount by which the antique collection exceeds the present value of the annuity, and this difference qualifies for a current charitable deduction. In effect, each annuity payment to you and your wife is composed of a return of capital (which is tax-free) and the balance of each payment is taxed as ordinary income. The major advantages of a gift annuity are the immediate charitable deduction, the assurance of life income for yourself and wife (part is tax-free), and the opportunity of not having to recognize a large capital gain.

In general, if you wish to make a charitable contribution and receive an annuity interest, you will be better off making the gift by a charitable remainder annuity trust rather than a gift annuity.

Seek counsel if you plan to use either of these techniques.

CHAPTER 18

Liquidating Collectibles

Liquidating antiques is not as easy as buying antiques. You can always find someone to sell you an antique. Buyers seem to disappear when you try to dispose of your beautiful "investments." Antiques can be liquidated; otherwise antiques would not be realistic investments. The manner of disposition depends upon several factors.

1. Return on your investment. How much are you trying to get from your antiques? Do not expect to make a "quick and dirty" sale and expect a large profit. Selling antiques for a "nice profit" takes time.
2. What are your cash flow needs? Do you need money now? If so, you may wish to dispose of the antiques at a reduced price. If your cash flow is anemic, such techniques as exchanging your antiques, using the installment method, or donating them to a charity are not for you.
3. What type of antiques are you trying to sell? Small items, large items, foreign, expensive, poor condition, etc.? The type of investment you have may dictate the manner of disposition.

4. What is your tax situation? High or low tax bracket, dealer or investor, hiding income? If you are in a high tax bracket, an installment sale, a non-taxable exchange, or a charitable disposition may be appropriate.
5. Your personal situation, your profession, and other variables may dictate the manner of disposition. For example, are you in a position to sell on credit? Does your position in your community necessitate that you must not try to sell the antique yourself?

Since each of you may need to dispose of your antiques, here is a brief list of possible sources. The items are not listed in any particular order.

1. Watch for "want to purchase" advertisements in the various antique publications and newspapers.
2. Run an advertisement to sell in a local newspaper or in various collectible publications. You will need an appraisal or certificate of a very high priced antique to sell to the general public. Your highest price may be gained with this approach; you are getting closer to retail prices. Some major publications are listed in the Appendix.

   Be careful if you are disposing of a valuable collection. Meet the individual in a bank or savings and loan association, if possible. Never take a small, expensive collection to an individual's home or business. Try to avoid letting them come to your home to see a collection. Small collectibles such as coins, stamps, and gems should be kept in a safe deposit box and not in your home. If antiques are sent through the mail, be sure to register them.
3. Sell the collection to a personal friend, a relative, or a business associate. With such a fiduciary relationship, a sale might go easier. Avoid sales to your employer or boss (for obvious reasons).
4. Profit share an antique collection with a dealer. Have the dealer purchase the collection with a latter sale with a 50:50 split. With a wholesale purchase, the return may be

A country cupboard, fashioned from cherrywood, which today might bring $700. Many people have inherited these and similar pieces, and may possibly have a preferential tax liability for the entire amount.

low. For single, high priced antiques your return on your investment may be high.

5. Establish a tailor-made marketing agreement with a retailer or wholesaler whereby you (the investor) provide the capital and the other party purchases and sells the antiques.
6. Sell your collection to a dealer, who may be found in the "Yellow Pages." This approach is more liquid, but the return may be low.
7. Trade-up your antiques. An investor may wish to trade a collectible for a more expensive item. For tax purposes, a trade is ideal since there is no tax on a trade of like-kind property where no boot is received by an investor.
8. Antiques may be sold at a bid board auction of a retail store. Obtain bid sheets and mount a photograph on them. The dealer's customers place bids on the sheets and the

highest bid prevails. The dealer will keep a commission from the sales (i.e., 20%).

9. Antiques may be sold at auction. After a commission is paid to the auction house, the return can be high. A list of auction houses is provided in the Appendix.
10. An investor can always sell a collection to a retail store, but the return on investment will often be low. An alternate approach is to consign the collection to the dealer. You name the price you wish, but the dealer may not try hard to sell the antiques. He may adopt a "stall" strategy hoping to "steal" the items if you become impatient. Be patient if you consign a collection.
11. If you are desperate, a collection may be sold to a pawnbroker or some other lending source. Do not expect a large profit. Use this source as a last resort.
12. A collection may be given to a charity. Be careful about picking an appropriate charity. Part of a charitable contribution deduction can be lost if a collection is given to a charity in which the antiques are unrelated to the exempt function of the charity.
13. Rather than selling a collection, it may be given to a relative (i.e., children). Tax savings may occur if the relative is in an overall lower tax bracket when the collection is finally sold. For example: give a highly appreciated collection to a child as he or she enters college. The child can sell the collection in order to pay college costs, and the gain is taxed in the child's lower tax bracket.
14. An individual may wish to retain an antique collection. Due to the operation of the tax laws, when the individual dies, his heirs can receive a "step-up in basis." In essence, the appreciation escapes the federal income tax. Keep in mind that an individual might use a collection for collateral at a bank in order to borrow money. Thus, you have the cash you need, you obtain an interest expense deduction, and the collection is appreciating in value. Is this not a tax shelter?

15. There is another possible technique—puts. A put is an individually tailored option which gives you the right to sell antiques to the writer of the contract at a stipulated price within a designated time.

    For example, you find a solvent individual (e.g., a dealer or broker) who is satisfactory to a bank or savings and loan. The broker binds himself to buy the antiques at your election during a certain period of time for a specific money premium. A bank might accept such a "put" as satisfactory collateral. Of course, if you do not ask the broker to buy the antiques within the stipulated timer, the broker retains the money premium and the option terminates.
16. For large collections, try bulk mailing to other potential buyers (dealers, professional people, etc.).
17. Purchase antiques for relatives and business associates. Here the antiques are pre-sold.
18. Sell your investments to a family member in return for fixed payments for your life. This private annuity technique is explained in Chapter 16.
19. Sell your antiques at nearby clubs. Put a notice in the club's publication or on the appropriate bulletin board. Many clubs have auctions frequently which may be another outlet to sell your antiques.

Yes, antiques can be sold, but you must work at it. You may obtain the profit which you believe you deserve, but if you have diversified your purchases, an overall profit can be obtained—*if antique prices continue to rise.* Before selling, these are some steps to take in order to obtain a higher price:

1. Your antiques should be arranged in a format which others can follow. Orderly albums and marked items are much easier for buyers to see and appreciate if, for example, you are involved with stamps.
2. Have an inventory of your collection with an estimate of net

value. Buyers need to know the price and quantities of your holdings.

3. You should describe the more valuable items in your collection. Most buyers are interested in the scarcer items.
4. Ascertain the true condition of your antiques. The quality of your collectibles will be a major factor in the pricing of your antiques.
5. Establish a realistic price for each item after considering condition, demand, and your personal cash needs.

CHAPTER 19

Using Antiques in Retirement Plans

Hard assets such as antiques, political campaign buttons, watches, rare stamps, and coins can be used in corporate pension plans, Keogh plans, and individual retirement accounts through 1981. See new law at end of this chapter.

If you work for an employer and contributions are being made to a qualified retirement plan on your behalf, ask your employer if such contributions may be invested in hard assets. Or if you are the owner of a closely-held corporation, arrange to have your corporate pension or profit-sharing plan to invest in high quality antiques. An incorporated professional individual such as a doctor, dentist, lawyer, accountant, etc., may find that deductible payments up to 15% of compensation to a corporate pension plan can be quite beneficial. Only employers and not employees receive deductions for contributions to qualified plans. But such contributions are not taxed to employees until received upon retirement or disability many years later. Furthermore, appreciation on the antiques is not taxable to the pension trust.

Self-employed individuals such as partners and sole proprietors are permitted to set up qualified retirement plans. Such plans may invest in hard assets. A self-employed obtains a current deduction from gross taxable income in the amount of the annual contribution to such a plan, but limited to the smaller of $15,000 ($7,500 before 1982) or 15% of earned income each year. Beginning in 1982, a participant in a Keogh plan may establish an IRA and make extra deductible contributions of up to $2,000 or make an additional contribution up to $2,000 to the Keogh plan.

For example, Johnson, a pharmacist on a calendar year and accrual basis, is the sole owner of a drugstore that nets him $45,000 per year. He sets up a profit-sharing trust for himself and two full-time non-seasonal employees who have been with him for more than three years. Their total compensation is $35,000. The plan calls for an annual contribution of 10 percent, rather than the permitted ceiling of 15 percent. Each year, Johnson must contribute $3,500 (10 percent of $35,000) to the plan for his two employees and then can contribute for his own benefit $4,150 (10 percent of $41,500 [$45,000 − $3,500]). Each participant may also place an additional $2,000 into the plan after 1981.

You may use a Keogh plan where you receive outside earned income other than from your employer. You may be a free-lance writer, operate a weekend plumbing service, an after-hours telephone service, or any other second employment. You can contribute up to 15% of this earned income to a Keogh plan even though you may participate in a corporate pension plan at your primary employment. Earned income refers to salary, professional fees, royalties, and sales, but does not include such passive income items as dividends or interest.

A contribution to a Keogh plan may be made up to April 15 and still qualify as a deduction for the previous year. But such Keogh plan must have been created by December 31 of the previous year in order to obtain a deduction for the prior year.

If you are not a member of a corporate retirement plan or a Keogh plan, all is not lost. A person can set up his own individual retirement account (IRA). To it he can contribute and deduct 100 percent (15% before 1982) of his compensation (or, in the case of a self-employed individual, his earned income) up to

There are about 10 trust institutions in the United States that allow hard assets in self-directed retirement plans. Stamps such as the 50¢ red violet (Scott #517) and the 50¢ green "Graf Zeppelin" (Scott #C-18) could be placed into corporate, Keogh, or Individual Retirement Accounts. However, a new law, if not repealed, will eliminate collectibles from self-directed retirement plans after 1981. (Photos courtesy of Harris Stamp Co., Boston, Massachusetts)

$2,000 ($1,500 before 1982) each year. If he is married and both spouses work, each can set up his or her own individual retirement account. If each of them earns at least $2,000, each can contribute up to $2,000 per year, a total of $4,000. Further, if only one spouse works, then that working spouse can elect instead to deduct up to $2,250 ($1,750 before 1982) per year to a spousal IRA.

There cannot be a joint account with the non-working spouse, but a subaccount with right of survivorship in the spouse is permitted. To be deductible the contribution can be made in that year or up to the date of filing the individual's tax return (including extensions).

For example, Mary Short has a yearly salary of $40,000 when she establishes an individual retirement account in 1982. She may contribute $2,000 to her account. If Mary Short has a non-employed spouse, she can contribute $2,250 for her spouse and herself.

Contributions to an IRA can be substantially increased through employer contributions. For tax years starting after December 31, 1981, an employer can contribute the smaller of $15,000 or 15 percent of the employee's earned income. The employee includes the contribution in gross income. Employer contributions must vest immediately. Where employer contributions are less than the normal limitations (i.e., lesser of $1,500 or 15 percent of earned income), the employee is allowed to contribute and deduct any difference. After 1981, an employee is allowed to contribute up to $2,000 to the SEP no matter what amount the employer contributes.

In the last example suppose Mary Short's employer establishes a written plan to make contributions to employee IRAs. Because Mary's yearly salary is $40,000, her employer could contribute up to $6,000 ($40,000 × .15) to her IRA. She could also contribute up to $2,000.

There are several organizations which will allow hard assets to be used in retirement plans. One such organization is First-Citizens Bank & Trust Company, P.O. Box 3028, Greenville, SC 29602. Contact them if you are interested in using high quality antiques in a corporate retirement plan, a Keogh plan, or an individual retirement account. Obtain a deduction for your antique purchases before 1982.

The recent tax bill signed into law by President Reagan in 1981 contains a "sleeper" which shall eliminate the use of antiques and other collectibles in IRAs, Keogh plans, and self-directed corporate retirement plans. Even if a collector or investor is not currently using collectibles in a retirement plan, it behooves you to write your Congressman and Senators to have this anti-free market provision repealed. If this new restrictive provision becomes effective on January 1, 1982, it probably will further depress the prices of most collectibles, including antiques.

Effective January 1, 1982, new Section 402(N) indicates that an acquisition by an individual retirement account or by an individually directed Keogh or corporate retirement account of any collectible shall be treated as a distribution from such account in an amount equal to the cost to such account of such collectible. This treatment as a distribution means that the taxpayer must pay a tax on the cost of the collectible just as if he had received cash from the plan. In other words, the taxpayer would lose the favorable tax deferred treatment associated with retirement plans.

A collectible is defined under this new law as any work of art, any rug or antique, any metal or gem, any stamp or coin, any alcoholic beverage, or any other tangible personal property that is specified by the Secretary of the Treasury.

Until December 31, 1981, collectors will be able to place antiques and other collectibles in IRA, Keogh, and self-directed plans. Although we will have to wait for regulations from the I.R.S., presumbly an individual will be able to invest in a limited partnership or trust which has been established to invest in collectibles. Further, fiduciaries and trustees of retirement plans should be allowed to invest other people's funds into antiques and other collectibles.

If you have an interest in your hobby, write those letters today to all appropriate lawmakers. This prohibition against antique items and other collectibles will have a significant negative impact upon our investment return in the very near future.

CHAPTER 20

Controversies with the I.R.S.

Since an employer must give each employee two (or three) copies of Form W-2 by January 31 of each calendar year, the employee should gather all pertinent information about his businesses including his antique activities and immediately prepare his return or have someone prepare it as soon as possible. The need for haste is two-fold. First, it will give the taxpayer time to gather additional information if needed. The second is more profitable. If a refund is due, then the sooner it is received the more valuable it is. Under present value analysis, a dollar today is worth more than a dollar next month. However, if money is owed, then the taxpayer may wish to wait until April to mail the return to the I.R.S.

Audit of Your Return

When the I.R.S. receives a tax return, it is checked by a computer for mathematical accuracy and completeness. A more sophisticated analysis called a Discriminant Function System (DIF) is also performed on the return. This analysis takes a set of values that the I.R.S. considers normal for someone with your income and number of dependents and compares these values with the claims made on your return. What the tests are and the values chosen are secret and in all probability these change from year to year. However, an awareness of the existence of the DIF make some steps advisable that might not be necessary otherwise.

To take a common example: If you earn $20,000 a year, then you probably live in a $60,000 house with a $50,000 mortgage at 12½% interest rate. Therefore, your home mortgage interest deduction should be (0.125 × $50,000) or $6,250.00. If you borrowed $5,000 at 20% for one year with your house as collateral, then the additional $1,000 in interest may make it appear that you own a $70,000 home, which is more than is average for your salary range.

The DIF system may kick out your return for closer inspection. The way to correct partially any DIF factors is to provide with the return additional information on any item that may appear abnormal. In the example above, attach a letter showing who the interest was paid to and itemize the amounts and note on your return at the appropriate place that a letter is attached. This simple step (if not taken to extremes) will allow the human examiner to quickly evaluate the cause for the DIF exception and if necessary a quick call will verify your deductions.

However, even without the DIF, there is always a chance that your return will be audited—in fact about 2% are audited each year. The higher the income and the more complicated the return, the greater the probability of an audit.

The audit procedure starts when the taxpayer is notified that his return is being examined and specifying whether an office or a field audit is to be made. There are two types of office audits—a correspondence audit and an office interview audit. As the name indicates, a correspondence audit means that some additional information is needed that can be supplied by mail. In the office interview audit, the taxpayer is asked to bring supporting records to the I.R.S. office where the interview takes place.

Field audits involve an agent coming to the business premises to conduct the audit. They are usually used for businesses and complex individual returns.

Two points need to be made. Never send or give original documents to an agent. Send a copy because the I.R.S. may lose the document.

If a *special agent* is conducting the audit, then the I.R.S. suspects fraud. Ask for identification and if a *special agent* is involved, obtain a lawyer immediately. Also, if you hear a special agent is checking your affairs, get a lawyer and retrieve any records from your accountant or any other non-lawyer tax advisor.

Small Claims Division of the Tax Court

If you and/or your advisor disagree with the I.R.S. audit and the amount involved is $5,000 or less, there is a special Small Tax Case Division of the Tax Court. This Small Tax Division simplifies tax disputes with the I.R.S. and gives taxpayers a better break.

Although the court must agree to hear your case, the only time the court can refuse is if the I.R.S. objects to the taxpayer's request on the grounds that important tax policies are involved and the question should be heard under normal procedures.

There are a number of advantages to this procedure. First, the taxpayer has only to complete a simple petition showing the I.R.S.'s alleged errors. Second, the trial generally will be closer to home since over 100 cities are used. Third, the time between petition and trial is shortened. Fourth, any evidence thought by the court to be of value is admissible and strict rules of evidence do not apply. Fifth, no brief is necessary unless the taxpayer chooses. Sixth, decisions are handed down more quickly than in regular cases. Seventh, the taxpayer may represent himself or may use a "non-tax specialist" to help him.

As in all other things, there are major disadvantages also. The decision is final. Neither the taxpayer nor the government may appeal. Nor can a precedent be created by any decision. Obviously the I.R.S. code is still the law to be applied.

How to Proceed

If you decide to use this procedure, the first step is to write the United States Tax Court, Box 70, Washington, DC 20044 and ask for the necessary information to file under the Small Tax Case Rules.

The necessary forms and an information booklet will be sent to the taxpayer.

After completion of the petition, the original and two copies should be mailed to the tax court along with a $60.00 check ($10.00 before 1982) made out to the "Treasurer of the United States." Warning: Since the petition and check must be mailed and postmarked prior to 90 days from the date of the notice of deficiency, the best procedure is to use certified mail and get a dated receipt from the post office.

CHAPTER 21

Insurance Protection

Insurance for your possessions, whether jewelry, antiques, or otherwise, is usually an individual matter that is best handled through your insurance broker. However, some general observations may be made that will aid you in assisting your broker to get the type and amount of coverage desired.

1. All items acquired should be appraised by a recognized authority. An appraisal is the essential first step in obtaining insurance. Periodic appraisals should be performed to monitor the progress of your collection.
2. Antiques are not generally recognized as a separate insurance category, as are, for example, silver, coins, and stamps. Therefore, antiques generally are protected under a broad category called Fine Arts. This broad category and the difficulty in defining antiques presents problems both to the insurance company and to the person desiring protection. For example, a Hepplewhite Roll-Top Desk (1803) would have little difficulty being insured, but a round oak table (1905) may create a problem. An extensive collection of Shirley Temple memorabilia would be quite valuable but might not be classified as Fine Arts.

Ordinary pedal-operated player pianos were a "give-away" item in quite recent times, but as this book is written (1981), one in good operating order will bring anywhere from $1,000 to $4,000, depending on where it is in the United States. (Photo courtesy of the Colorado Springs Gazette-Telegraph*)*

An important and highly desirable provision in some policies concerning Fine Arts coverage is that new acquisitions are automatically covered up to a given percentage of your coverage, provided the insured reports such objects within a given number of days after acquisition.

3. Fire protection is usually easy to get but theft protection is more difficult.
4. Protection for items stored away from your home is very hard to obtain and probably will be limited to a fixed percentage of the insurance on your home contents. Again the type of protection desired will dictate the ease with which it can be obtained.

CHAPTER 22

Leveraging

The major advantage of most tax shelters is the concept of leveraging. Leveraging is the use of other people's money to invest. If you are paying off a mortgage on a home, you are leveraging. Further, the interest expense and real estate taxes are deductible. You have borrowed the money and still enjoy the benefits of living in your home. Another example of leveraging is the stockholder who purchases stock on the "margin." He purchases $100,000 of stock and pays only $30,000 down. Of course, if the stock goes down, there may be margin calls wherein the stockholder has to provide more money. The commodity market is, of course, based upon this leveraging concept.

Let us take an example in real estate to see the benefit of this type of strategy. Suppose you purchase a piece of raw land for $100,000, paying down $20,000. After one year goes by, you sell the land for $120,000. Ignoring your interest costs, your return on investment is 100%.

$$\frac{\$\ 20{,}000}{20{,}000} = 100\%$$

Late Sheraton dressing bureau of highly figured maple. A typical price of this, as this book is written, could be $450. (Photo courtesy of Mapes Auctioneers/ Appraisers, Vestal, New York)

Whereas, if you had paid cash for the land, your return on your investment would only be 20%.

$$\frac{\$\ 20{,}000}{100{,}000} = 20\%$$

If you were able to find an astute banker, a leverage strategy could be developed with antique investments. Here are the investment and tax advantages of a "leveraged antique investment." Suppose you purchased some ancient coins for $100,000, quite possibly at auction. You borrow $80,000 from a bank in order to finance the purchase, with the amount due in three (3) years with an 11% interest rate. The bank would retain the coin(s) for collateral purposes. Avoid borrowing money from a coin firm by paying off the rare coin through an installment method. There have been too many cases of silver and coin firms going out of business and leaving you holding an empty bag. You should take possession and then use the rare coins as collateral.

Your interest deduction would be $8,800 per year, or $26,400 for the three years. However, if you are in the 50% bracket, your deduction each year brings your total cost down to $13,200 (.50 × $26,400). Suppose the ancient coins are sold at auction three years later for $130,000 (less commissions). You have earned $16,800 ($30,000 − 13,200) of profit, with a return on your investment of 66% or 22% per year (before any capital gain tax). You pay off the note, pocket $16,800 (before tax) and the banker has earned $26,400 of interest income.

Do not expect many bankers to jump at this interesting tax shelter. The best bet would be a banker who is also a believer in hard assets. Bankers are a conservative lot, but they loan money on real estate. Yet rare coins and antiques are probably more liquid than real estate. If there are any banker-readers out there who might be interested in loaning money in such a leverage technique, please drop either author a note!

Other References

Crumbley, *A Practical Guide to Preparing a Federal Gift Tax Return,* Lawyers & Judges Publishing Co., P. O. Box 42050, Tucson, AZ 85733, 1980, $8.50.

Crumbley, *A Practical Guide to Preparing a Federal Estate Tax Return,* 1980, Lawyers & Judges Publishing Co., P. O. Box 42050, Tucson, AZ 85733, $8.50.

Crumbley, *Financial Management of Your Coin/Stamp Estate,* Information Services, P. O. Box 9027, College Station, TX 77840.

Crumbley & Davis, *Organizing, Operating, & Terminating Subchapter S Corporations,* Lawyers & Judges Publishing Co., P. O. Box 42050, Tucson, AZ 85733, $29.50.

Dacey, *How to Avoid Probate Updated,* $14.95, Probate, Naugatuck, CT 06770.

Gilbert, *Investing in The Antique Market,* Grosset & Dunlap, Inc., 51 Madison Avenue, New York, NY 10010.

How To Survive and Prosper in the Next American Depression, War, or Revolution, Financial Management Associates, Inc., 3824 East Indian School, School Road, Phoenix, AZ 85018.

McCarthy, Crumbley, and Davis, *The Federal Income Tax: Its Sources and Applications,* Prentice-Hall, Inc., Englewood Cliffs, NJ 07632, $20.95.

Milam and Crumbley, *Estate Planning After the 1976 Tax Reform Act,* AMACOM, 135 West 50th Street, New York, NY 10020, $14.50.

Sommer, *How to Make Money in the Antique and Collectibles Business,* $10.95, Houghton Mifflin Company, 2 Park Street, Boston, MA 02107.

Some Auction Houses

1. Sotheby Parke Bernet, 980 Madison Avenue, New York, NY 10021.
2. Investment Rarities, Inc., One Appletree Street, Minneapolis, MN 55420.
3. Bowers and Ruddy Galleries, Suite 600, 6922 Hollywood Blvd., Los Angeles, CA 90028. (coins)
4. Stack's, 123 W. 57th Street, New York, NY 10019. (coins)
5. Robert A. Siegel, 120 East 56th Street, New York, NY 10022.
6. Christie, Manson & Woods, 502 Park Avenue, New York, NY 10022.
7. William Doyle, 175 E. 87th Street, New York, NY 10028.
8. Butterfield & Butterfield, 1244 Sutter Street, San Francisco, CA 94109.
9. Christie's East, 219 E. 67th Street, New York, NY 10021.
10. Phillips, 867 Madison Avenue, New York, NY 10021.
11. Robert Skinner, Route 117, Bolton, MA 01740.
12. C. G. Sloan Co., 715 13 St. N.W., Washington, DC 20005.
13. Earl P. L. Apfelbaum, Inc., 1819 John F. Kennedy Blvd., Suite 201, Philadelphia, PA 19103.
14. Samuel T. Freeman, 1808 Chestnut St., Philadelphia, PA 19103.

Some Suggested Periodicals

American Art and Antiques, Billboard Publications, 1515 Broadway, New York, NY 10036.

Antique Collecting, Box 327, Ephrata, PA 17522.

Antique Gazette, 929 Davidson Dr., Nashville, TN 37205.

Antiques and Auction News, Box 225, W. Market St., Marietta, PA 17547.

Antiques, Straight Enterprises, 551 Fifth Ave., New York, NY 10017.

Antiques Dealer, Ebel-Doctorow Publishers, Inc., 1115 Clifton Ave., Clifton, NJ 07013.

Antiques World, 112 E. 42 St., New York, NY 10017.

Art Letter, 150 E. 58 St., New York, NY 10022.

Art News, 122 E. 42 St., New York, NY 10017.

Coin World, Amos Press, Inc., Sidney, OH 45365.

Collector Editions Quarterly, 170 Fifth Ave., New York, NY 10010.

Collector's Guide, City Magazines, Ltd., 1–3 Wine Office Court, Fleet St., London, EC4A 3A1, England.

Collector/Investor, 740 Rush St., Chicago, IL 60611.

Collector's Journal, Box 601, Vinton, IA 52349.

Collectors News, 606 8th Ave., Grundy Center, IA 50638.

Connoisseur, National Magazine Co. Ltd., England, 250 W. 55 St., New York 10019.

Gray Letter, P. O. Drawer 2, Tuscaloosa, AL 35401.

Hard Facts, Box 287, Cardiff, CA 92007.

Hobbies, 10006 So. Michigan Ave., Chicago, IL 60605.

Inside View, Box 6125, Huntington Beach, CA 92646.

International Art Market, pub. by *Art in America,* 150 E. 58 St., New York, NY 10002.

Kovels on Antiques and Collectibles, Box 222000, N. Beachwood, OH 44122.

Old Cars, Krause Publications, Iola, WI 54945.

Personal Finance, 901 N. Washington St., Alexandria, VA 22314.

Plate Collector, Box 981, Kermit, TX 79745.

PreciouStone Newsletter, P. O. Box 4649, Thousand Oaks, CA 91359.

Spinning Wheel, American Antiques and Craft Society, Fame Ave., Hanover, PA 17331.

Stamp Collector, Box 10, Albany, OR 97321.

Index